Samuel T. Davis

Caribou shooting in Newfoundland

With a History of England's oldest Colony from 1001 to 1895

Samuel T. Davis

Caribou shooting in Newfoundland
With a History of England's oldest Colony from 1001 to 1895

ISBN/EAN: 9783337059606

Printed in Europe, USA, Canada, Australia, Japan

Cover: Foto ©ninafisch / pixelio.de

More available books at **www.hansebooks.com**

CARIBOU SHOOTING

IN

NEWFOUNDLAND:

WITH A HISTORY OF ENGLAND'S OLDEST COLONY
FROM 1001 TO 1895.

BY

S. T. DAVIS, M. D.

(SHONGO.)

——— —— · ——

LANCASTER, PA.
THE NEW ERA PRINTING HOUSE.
1895.

TO

My Venerable Father,

HENRY DAVIS,

WHO IN HIS EIGHTY-SECOND YEAR

IS STILL

THE ARDENT SPORTSMAN

FROM WHOM I EARLY LEARNED TO LOVE

THE ROD AND GUN,

THIS NARRATIVE IS DEDICATED

AS A

SLIGHT EXPRESSION OF THE FILIAL AFFECTION

OF THE AUTHOR.

PREFACE.

INDFUL of the time and patience required in finding out a very little about this picturesque island before setting out for its distant shores, and of the uncertainty which surrounded every movement after the start was made, as well as the unnecessary expense incurred for want of a reliable itinerary, we conceived the idea of furnishing in compact form just the information our party was most anxious to secure, and only obtained at an exorbitant price, and after repeated disappointments.

Our historical notes were largely gathered from an excellent little work entitled "Newfoundland as it is in 1894," by the acknowledged historian of the Island, Rev. M. Harvey, of St. John's, whose appended letter explains itself:

ST. JOHN'S, N. F., December 10th, 1894.

DEAR DOCTOR DAVIS :—I am very much pleased to learn that you intend publishing an account of your experiences in Newfoundland. That is what we want—to make the country known. You are heartily welcome to use my book in any way you please, and to any extent.

Sincerely yours,
M. HARVEY.

Most of the illustrations of the trip were made from photographs taken in the field by the author; those showing the specimens are by Mr. B. Frank Saylor, of Lancaster. The heads were mounted by Messrs. A. C. Wood, of Painted Post, New York, and George Flick, of Lancaster. A glance at the illustrations themselves is sufficient to testify to the faithful work of all parties engaged upon subjects and pictures.

Careful daily notes were taken, and are the basis of the story of the hunt, which is rather understated than overdrawn. If any brother hunter has a doubt of this he has only to profit by our experience and try it for himself. If this little work shall encourage other brain workers to find rest and healthful recreation in this interesting region, our effort will not have been in vain, and their pleasure will be the best reward of

THE AUTHOR.

CONTENTS.

LIST OF ILLUSTRATIONS.

CARIBOU SHOOTING IN NEWFOUNDLAND.

CHAPTER I.

Outings a Necessity to Brain Workers—"Can't Afford It"—
How to Raise the Wind—Transmute Smoke into Gold—
Consolidate your "Days off," and Have Something to
Show for Them—Longer Life and More in It.

WHILE the forests and fauna of the North
American continent steadily decrease from
year to year, the army of "outers" and so-
called sportsmen increases still more rapidly—from
Presidents occupying the highest office in the gift of
the people, to farmers' sons—through all the learned
professions and tradespeople—rounding up with the
"pot" or market hunter who kills both in and out of
season, whenever and wherever an opportunity offers.

For the past twenty years it has been the author's
custom to take an outing of from four to six weeks
every year; and for various reasons he has pitched
his tent or built his cabin or lean-to in many sections
of our great country. In all of these delightful trips

2   (9)

he has been accompanied by from one to three boon
companions, and the localities visited have ranged
from the interior of Newfoundland in the north to the
sand-dunes and palmetto swamps washed by the warm
waters of the Gulf in the south, and westward to the
shores of the placid Pacific.

As these pilgrimages have extended into seventeen
States and Territories and the Dominion of Canada,
he has learned much from practical experience with
regard to the haunts and habits of our native game
and fishes—from the ungainly moose, noble elk and
caribou, to the diminutive chipmunk, and from the
Silver King to the sprightly sunfish. The note-book
and camera have always been close companions, and
as Time's wheels roll on they afford much pleasure,
in recalling to mind many incidents of our sports
afield.

Born and reared as he was among the mountains of
central Pennsylvania, where half a century ago game
was plentiful, and where, under the tutelage of his
now venerable father—who is yet an ardent sportsman, though in his eighty-second year—he learned
the use of the rod and gun at a very tender age. Is
it any wonder, then, that when the sap begins to fall
and the leaves to change color in the autumn, he becomes restless under the yoke of arduous professional

duties, and anxious to seek "the habitat of fin, fur and feather"—there to break that fatal strain on the nervous system from the daily routine of work and worry which has hurried so many good men to premature graves.

HINTS TO BRAIN-WORKERS.

If brain-workers as a class would take less "nervines," clubs and banquets, and stick to three square meals a day of well-cooked, healthful food, with an outing of from four to six weeks out of the fifty-two, the country at large would be benefited, and we would have better lawyers, doctors and divines, brighter students and more successful merchants.

It would be improper in the introduction to this narrative to dwell at length upon the importance of out-door sports to brain-workers, and indeed to all whose pursuits require them to draw upon nerve force, especially in-doors, day in and out, like automata. The unanimous verdict is stereotyped and familiar to all that "all work and no play makes Jack a dull boy."

"Yes," said a friend since my return, "I would enjoy an outing to Newfoundland to the fullest extent, and would be benefited in many ways. I, too, love the rippling brook, the majestic river, real land-

scapes, towering mountains, the pure bracing atmosphere, and to float on the ocean waves; but alas! I
cannot afford such an outing. It is not 'too rich for
my blood,' but for my purse—there's the rub. I get
just that far, and the barrier is so great that, crest-
fallen, I give up in despair, and take a day off here
and there. Three or four times during the summer I
go to the river for a day's fishing for bass, and as often
I run down to the beach, spending one or two days at
a time there. This, with an occasional shoot with the
club at inanimate targets, makes up about all the recreation I can afford, unless you can put me on a plan
by which I can take a better outing—conscious as I
am of the fact that the 'day at a time' outing is of
very little benefit, inasmuch as I must work all the
harder to make up for the day or two of temporary
absence." Knowing my friend's income, habits, home
life and inclinations, as well as his oft-expressed desire
to accompany me on one of my annual outings, I was
not long in obtaining his permission to be inter-
viewed, and assured of correct replies to such questions as I might ask, with a view of his "raising the
wind," and enabling him to take an outing from
which he could derive some permanent benefit.

"Ready? Here goes! How many extra or unne-
cessary meals do you take and pay for at the club or

restaurant during the course of a year, and what do they cost?"

"At a low estimate fifty, and at a cost of not less than seventy-five cents each."

"Fifty meals at seventy-five cents each equal $37.50. Do you smoke, and if so what?"

"Yes, I smoke four ten-cent cigars a day."

"Well, as a rule, the difference between a ten-cent cigar and one for five cents, as they are found in the market, is simply the difference in the price. If you must smoke four cigars a day, cast about and save twenty cents a day, or seventy-three dollars a year, by smoking a good five-cent cigar. Or, better still, one dozen Creme Gambier French clay pipes will cost fifty cents; six cents will purchase sufficient rubber tubing to tip the stems; one pound of Vindex or Seal of North Carolina smoking tobacco will fill your pipe four times a day for forty days, and ten pounds will last you a year, at an expense of about five dollars and fifty-five cents, saving on the cigar-smoking at forty cents a day $140.45, or if you buy them at wholesale, say $100.00 on this one 'extra.' And by using either of these brands of smoking tobacco you will have a milder, sweeter smoke than you can possibly obtain from the general run of cigars, and with vastly less enervating effect on the general health;

besides, you escape the dangers lurking in the small
end of the cigar (unless you use a smoker).

"Now, you say you take a day off about four times
a summer to go bass-fishing. On an average, what
does it cost you on one of those trips?"

"Well, railroad fare or horse hire, boatman, bait,
etc., about $5.00 a day, or $20.00 a year."

"And four times in the season you run down to the
seashore, which takes two days each trip, or eight
days in all. What do those trips cost?"

"Well, about $15.00 each, or $60.00 for the year."

"Now, my friend, I know you take a glass of
whiskey occasionally, and that you take your beer in
the evening. Give me some idea of what you expend
for drinks for self and friends."

"Well, I will frankly say that I kept a memoran-
dum once for several months, and was astonished to
find that I was paying out on an average fifty cents a
day, or about $180.00 a year, for my drink habit."

"Unless you are very sure that you are much benefited by this outlay, you would do well to consider the
propriety of investing the same amount in some other
enterprise, and I would suggest that it be added to
the outing fund.

"This is not all; you inform me that you are a
member of a gun club. How often do you shoot

with it, and on an average how much does each shoot cost you?"

"I shoot, I presume, on an average, about ten times a year, and after I pay for shells and incidentals, including losses in races in which the other fellow hits oftener than I do, say five dollars, or $50.00 a year."

"Let's see what this all amounts to: $37.50 for extra meals during the year; $100.00 for smoking; $20.00 for fishing; $60.00 for trips to the shore; $180.00 for drinks, and $50.00 for the shooting club — making a total of $447.50, or nearly $1.25 for each day in the year. This is the way money goes for that for which we have nothing to show. I have been there, and as you see, know just how it is. I also know that from $250.00 to $300.00, if properly expended, will defray all the expenses of a grand outing of from six weeks to two months to any point in the United States, Canada or Newfoundland, and with all the advantages and comforts of first-class travel, leaving a balance for extras and some trophies of the chase which money could not purchase, and which are ever a source of pleasure and instruction as specimens of Natural History, and positive evidence of one's prowess and skill with the gun.

"Now, my friend, you see where the money comes from which pays the expenses of my outings. You

drop on an average $1.25 a day in having what is
generally considered to be a good time, and in what
the boys call 'sowing their wild oats.' Try dropping
80 cents into your outing fund, and at the end of the
year you will have the comfortable sum of $292.00,
out of which you can get more solid fun and grand
sport in the Island of Newfoundland than ever you
dreamed of, and you will still have forty-five cents a
day for creature comforts—which is found to be ample
for a goodly number of the outing fraternity, and is
as much and even more than thousands of good, in-
dustrious citizens earn."

It is to be hoped that the reader will not be led to
think that the author is posing as a reformer, from
this prelude to the description of an outing which for
variety and satisfactory results eclipsed any among
the many in years gone by. At the same time, it does
none of us any harm to have our little shortcomings
alluded to, and especially where experience has proven
the correctness of the criticism; for there is scarcely
any doubt that many of those who peruse these pages
will recognize the picture in this introduction, and if
but few do as the author has long since done—change
front—the battle may last longer, but the outcome
will be more satisfactory, and certainly the outings
will be more numerous and beneficial.

CHAPTER II.

Its Geographical Position—Comparative Size—Form—Coast Aspect—The Interior—Mountain Chains—Rivers—Lakes and Ponds—Bays.

HAVING endeavored to convince the reader of the value, even necessity, of an occasional outing to the prolongation and enjoyment of life, he is now to be made acquainted with the scene of our last, and in many respects most successful experiment in that line—the Island of Newfoundland.

The world in general outside of this, the tenth in size of the islands of the world, knows but little of it; and if graduates of high schools and academies were to be required to tell all they know about it the answer would be limited to its geographical position, number of square miles, something about the banks, codfish, seals, snow, ice and fog; and perhaps inform you that the capital is, or was, St. John's.

Newfoundland is England's oldest colony, and lies off the east coast of North America, and directly across the Gulf of St. Lawrence. Its southwestern extremity approaches within 50 miles of Cape Breton, while its most easterly projection is but 1640 miles from Valentia, on the coast of Ireland. It is situated between 46° 36′ 50″ and 51° 39′ north latitude, and between 52° 37′ and 59° 24′ 50″ west longitude. Its greatest length, from Cape Ray to Cape

ST. JOHN'S, THE CAPITAL.

Norman, is 317 miles; its greatest breadth, from Cape Spear to Cape Anguille, 316 miles; and its total area about 42,000 square miles. The best idea of its extent is obtainable by comparison with other countries with which we are familiar. For example, it is almost as large as the State of New York, twice the size of Nova Scotia, one-third larger than New Brunswick, one-sixth larger than Ireland, three times as large as Holland, and twice as large as Denmark. Its figure roughly approaches an equilateral triangle. (See map.) Two large peninsulas project from the main body of the island : one of these (Petit Nord) points northwards, and is long and narrow; the other is the peninsula of Avalon, pointing southeast, and almost severed from the mainland — the connection being a narrow isthmus, in one place but three miles wide. On the eastern side of the peninsula of Avalon is situated St. John's, the capital.

THE COAST.

As seen from the ocean, the shores of Newfoundland furnish a picture of rock-bound cliffs rising from 200 to 500 feet in height, broken by numerous magnificent bays, running in some instances 80 to 90 miles inland and throwing out smaller arms in all directions, so that though the circumference of the island from headland to headland is about 1000 miles, the actual length of coast line is more than twice as much. These bays frequently present varied scenes of beauty, being studded with small islands, having their shores clad in many instances with dark green forests to the water's edge, while in others the rocks are barren or moss-covered.

THE INTERIOR.

The part of the island nearest the sea consists of a hilly country, with eminences of no very great elevation. The interior proper consists as a whole of an

ENTRANCE TO SALVAGE HARBOR.

elevated undulating plateau, traversed here and there by ranges of low hills; the surface being diversified with valleys, woods, fresh-water lakes and ponds, and thousands of acres of marshes. All the great hill ranges take a northeasterly and southwesterly direction, the highest land occurring along the western and southern shores. The principal mountain chain is the Long Range, which extends along the western side of the island for nearly its entire length, and has peaks more than 2,000 feet high. Parallel to this, but nearer the coast, is the Cape Anguille range. The peninsula of Avalon is very hilly, but the highest summits do not extend 1,500 feet.

RIVERS.

The largest river is the Exploits, which is 200 miles in length, with a drainage area of between 3,000 and 4,000 square miles. It has its source in the extreme southwestern angle of the island, and flows in a north-easterly direction through Red Indian Lake, discharging its waters into the Bay of Exploits Notre Dame. The Grand Fall of the Exploits is nineteen miles up the river. The first plunge is fifty feet, the stream being separated on the verge of the precipice by a small island, and at the bottom pent up in a narrow tortuous gorge, hemmed in by craggy cliffs. The valley through which the river flows contains large areas of fertile land, much of which is covered with pine forests containing timber of large size.

The next river in size is the Humber, which has its source twenty miles inland from Bonne Bay and after a very circuitous route discharges its waters into Deer

Lake, thence flowing into the Bay of Islands. It drains an area of 2,000 square miles.

The Gander river is the next in size, and rises near the southern coast, flowing through Gander Lake, discharging into Gander Bay on the east coast, and has a drainage area of 2,500 square miles.

GRAND FALL OF THE EXPLOITS.

FRESH WATER LAKES AND PONDS.

These form one of the most remarkable physical features of this unique region, and occupy nearly one-third of the whole surface. The largest is Grand Lake, 56 miles in length and covering an area of 196 square miles. It contains an island 22 miles in length and 5 miles in width. Red Indian Lake is 37 miles long and 64 square miles in area. Gander Lake and Deer Lake occupy 33 and 24 square miles respectively. Sandy Lake, Victoria, Hinds, Terra Nova and George IV. Lakes rank next in size. The shores of many of these lakes, as well as the fertile valleys through

SCENE ON GRAND LAKE.

which the rivers flow, are as yet absolute solitudes, the very existence of which was until recently almost unknown.

THE BAYS.

Of the many bays already alluded to, the following deserve special mention:

St. Mary's Bay is 25 miles wide at its mouth and 35 miles long, with two great arms, Salmonier and Colinet, both of which stretch still farther into the interior. Placentia Bay is 55 miles wide and 90 miles long. Fortune Bay is 25 miles wide and 70 in length, with numerous arms, the most important of which are Bay D'Espoir, Hermitage Bay and Connaigre Bay.

At the entrance of Fortune Bay are the two islands of St. Pierre and Miquelon, ceded by treaty to France for the shelter of her fishermen, and now all that remains to France of the vast possessions she once held in North America, and this she holds to the great detriment of the Newfoundlanders.

Around Bay St. George, which is 40 miles wide at its mouth, with a good harbor at its head, are some of the most fertile valleys on the island, with fine forests of timber and coal-fields of large area. Bay of Islands has three fine arms running 20 miles inland, and here is located an extensive herring fishery.

Notre Dame Bay is 50 miles wide at its mouth, and runs inland 80 miles. On its shores are famous copper mines which have been worked with marked success, as well as the Pilley's Island Pyrites mine, which is now being worked at a great profit to the syndicate owning the plant. Pilley's Island is in the mouth of Notre Dame Bay and the point from which an arm known as Hall Bay extends 25 miles into the interior in a southwesterly direction. Our expedition left the ship at this point, and reached the White Hills from the head of Hall's Bay.

S. S. AVALON TAKING PYRITES ORE AT PILLEY'S ISLAND.

3

CHAPTER III.

HE FAUNA of Newfoundland will be next briefly touched upon. Among the indigenous animals, the Woodland (*Rangifer Caribou*) Caribou or Reindeer holds a conspicuous place, as the island contains more of these noble animals than any other country in the world. They migrate regularly to the southeastern and northwestern portions of the island, passing the winter months in the south, where "browse" is plentiful and the snow not too deep to prevent them from obtaining the moss and lichens on the lower grounds and upon which they principally feed the year round. In March they begin their spring migration to the mountains and barrens of the northwest where, in May and June, they bring forth their young. As soon as the forests of October begin to nip the vegetation, they begin to

graze toward the south; hence from the middle of
September until the same time in November is the
best time for stalking, when at times they can be seen

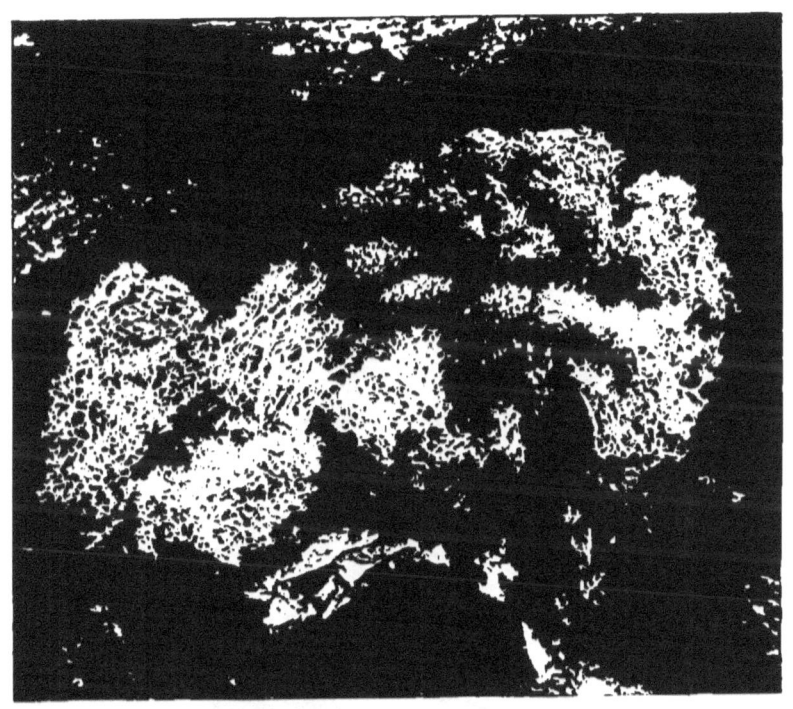

WHITE GROUND CARIBOU MOSS UPON WHICH THEY FEED IN THE
ABSENCE OF SNOW.

on the marshes in great herds, containing frequently
more than a hundred. The time of migration depends somewhat on the frosts and snows in the north,
as an early snow will cause the deer to start; but if

the weather becomes warm they call a halt and remain in the neighborhood where the warm weather
sets in, and at times they graze northward, resuming

BLACK CARIBOU MOSS AS IT OCCURS ON TREE TRUNKS AND
BRANCHES.   WINTER FOOD WHEN SNOW IS DEEP.

their southward journey when the weather becomes colder.

There are bears, wolves and other animals, in addition to the caribou, which is the only member of the deer family on the island. The black bear and wolf are abundant in the interior, especially the former, and in addition the black, grey, silver and red fox; also beaver, otter, Arctic hare, North American hare, weasel, bat, rat, mouse and muskrat. The famous Newfoundland dog is still to be met with, though good specimens are few and far between, and those expecting to make a purchase had better consult one of the many kennels in the United States, where there is an opportunity of making a selection. The Newfoundland dog of to-day is a degenerate mongrel, good for nothing except to drag a heavy clog during the summer, and the sledge during the winter months. There are no frogs, toads, snakes, lizards or any other reptiles on the island.

BIRDS.

It is estimated that there are 300 species of birds in the island, most of which are migratory. Among them are the eagle, hawk, owl, woodpecker, swallow, kingfisher, six species of flycatchers and a like number of thrushes, warblers, finches, ravens and jays.

The ptarmigan, or willow grouse, is very abundant
and is the finest game bird on the island.   They are
about the size of the pheasant or ruffled grouse of the

FEMALE.   MALE.

PTARMIGAN OR WILLOW GROUSE IN MOTTLED COAT FALL OF YEAR.

States, though not such rapid flyers, and furnish fine
sport, and their flesh is all that could be wished for—
juicy, sweet and tender.   In summer they are of a
reddish brown, but in winter almost white, with

feathers to their toe nails. The rock ptarmigan is found in the highest and most barren portions of the island, though not in such great numbers as the willow grouse or ptarmigan, which is found in all parts.

FLORA.

The pine, spruce, birch, juniper and larch of the forests in the interior furnish ample material for a large lumber trade, as well as for shipbuilding purposes. The white pine grows from a height of from seventy to eighty feet in some sections, and attains a diameter of from three to four feet. The mountain ash, balsam poplar and aspen thrive well, and evergreens are in endless variety.

The Geological Report of the Gander River district estimates the available pine limits here at 850 square miles, including the valley of the Gambo and Triton River and the country along the south side of the lake and across to Freshwater Bay. Most, if not all, the pine here referred to is of the white variety— *Pinus strobus*—probably the most valuable species for the manufacture of lumber. The same authority says that between the Grand Falls and Badger Brook on both sides of the Exploits River pine flourishes luxuriantly; these reaches also display a fine growth of other varieties of timber, and at some points, and especially above the forks of Sandy Brook, white birch attains a very large size.

The southern side of the Exploits presents an unbroken dense forest in a series of gentle undulations for many miles, and from the Victoria River to the head of Red Indian Lake the country is well timbered throughout.

The valley of the Humber is richly wooded, and here lumbering operations have been carried on for many years on an extensive scale. Here Tamarack or juniper, yellow birch, white pine and spruce grow in profusion, and to a size very little inferior if not equal to the best that is now brought to market at Gaspe and other parts of the Lower Province of Canada.

Berry-bearing plants are found distributed over the whole of the island and in great variety, among which may be mentioned strawberries, raspberries, capillaire, partridge berries, bakeapple and "hurtz" or blueberries, which can be gathered in the immediate vicinity of every settlement.

CHAPTER IV.

THE FISHERIES.

Abundance of Trout and Salmon—" No Fish" except the Cod, in Native Parlance—Codfish the Staple Export—Volume of the Business—A Permanent Industry—Arctic Current slime feeds the small fishes, they feed the Cod, the Cod feeds Man—Seal Fisheries—Slaughter of the "Harps"—The Sealing Gun—Distance measured by "Gunshots"—Salmon —Herring—Lobster.

ERHAPS there is no place on this earth where fishes are as plentiful as in and around Newfoundland. In every rivulet, river, lake, pond or puddle of water, no matter where found, trout and salmon abound, and in season the angler cannot fail to get a strike and is ofttimes rewarded with six to seven pound "speckled beauties," and salmon weighing as much as fifteen pounds. These fish, coming out of the pure cold spring water with rock bottom, are of superior flavor; but fine as they are, the natives do not regard them as fish, as the following incident will illustrate. On our way into the interior, part of our route was over a lovely pond five miles long by about three-fourths of a mile wide. We had

made an early start and left the foot of the pond just as day was breaking. We had not proceeded far when the writer thought he could occasionally see the water break with a splash in close proximity to the canoe. Seated as he was in the bow, he turned to the native who was handling the paddle in the stern, and inquired whether there were any fish in the pond. " Fish? No sir,— no fish, sir." Presently, when about half way up the pond, and just as the sun was peeping over the eastern horizon, he saw not six feet from the bow of the canoe a magnificent salmon rise to the surface, and with a swish of his tail, disappear to the depths. Again he turned to his friend with the remark, "Daddy, did I understand you to say that there were no fish in this pond?" "No Fish, sir; no fish." "Yes, but—I beg your pardon—I a moment ago saw what I took to be a twelve or fifteen pound salmon break the water not six feet from the bow of the canoe." " Oh, that was a salmon. There are plenty of trout and salmon in all these waters, but no fish, sir. You know we don't count anything as fish in these parts but codfish, sir."

CODFISH.

The fisheries of Newfoundland are the grand staple industry of the country, and about four-fifths of the entire exports. The cod fisheries alone greatly exceed those of any other country in the world. The annual average export of this valuable fish is about 1,350,000 quintals of 112 pounds weight. The Dominion of Canada exports an average of 450,000 quintals and

HARVEST TIME ON THE BANKS.

Norway 751,000 quintals. The whole Norwegian catch averages 50,000,000 codfish, while the aggregate annual catch of cod in North American waters, including the fisheries on the banks by French, American, Canadian and Newfoundland fishermen is estimated at 3,700,000 quintals. The number of codfish captured to make up this weight of dried fish, allowing fifty to a quintal, would be 185,000,000; and yet this enormous annual draft on these extensive fishing grounds has been going on for centuries without exhausting the supply.

A PERMANENT INDUSTRY.

The Arctic Current, which washes the shores of Labrador and Newfoundland, is laden with food on which the cod lives and thrives, and brings with it a never-failing supply for its sustenance. So far from being unfavorable to the production of life, the Arctic seas and the great rivers which they send forth are swarming with minute forms of life, constituting in many places "a living mass, a vast ocean of living slime." Swarms of minute crustaceans, annelids, and mollusca feed on this slime and in their turn become food for the larger marine animals even up to the giant whale; and curiously enough, this ocean slime is most abundant in the coldest waters, and especially in the neighborhood of ice-fields and icebergs. Thus the great current in the ocean, which rushes out of Baffin Bay, carrying on its bosom myriads of icebergs and washing the shores of Labrador and Newfoundland, is swarming with these minute forms of marine life from the minute crustacean and the crab and prawn together, with the molluscous animals and star-

fish in profusion, which contribute to the support of
the great schools of cod which find their home there.
Astounding are these great processes of nature! The
vast battalions of icebergs, the terror of mariners,
sailing past these shores and often anchoring on Labrador and in the bays of Newfoundland, bring with

CURING COD AT HARBOR BRITON.

them the slime food on which the almost microscopic
crustaceans live. These in turn furnish food for the
caplin, the squid and the herring, which with multi-
tudes of other species are food for the voracious cod.
When the cod is assimilated by man this great circle is
complete: the big fishes devour the little fishes, and we
have another evidence of the "survival of the fittest."

So long as the Arctic Current continues to flow, the banks and the waters about the island of Newfoundland will teem with cod. For nearly 400 years, cod fishing has been prosecuted regularly, and has supplied the chief export of the country. The fish begin to appear on the coast about the first of June, at which time they leave the deep water for the warmer and shallower waters near shore to deposit their spawn. Their approach is heralded by the beautiful trim little caplin, a fish about seven inches long and which comes in schools sufficient to give the water the appearance of a squirming mass, filling every nook and corner in the bays, fiords, arms and interstices of the rock-bound coast. The cod follow in their wake and gorge themselves with the little fish, of which they are very fond, so they furnish the choicest bait. In about six weeks the caplin disappear and their place is taken by the squid about the first of August. They are followed by the herring, which remain until about the middle or end of October, when the cod fishing season ends.

THE SEAL FISHING.

Next to the cod fishing in value comes that of the seal, which has been prosecuted for about ninety years only—the natives being so industriously engaged in cod fishing that they neglected the oleaginous treasures to be obtained from the seal, which the ice-fields yearly brought within their reach; so the great herds were left to bring forth their young amid the icy solitudes, undisturbed by the murderous gun, club and knife of the seal hunters. To-day, however, things are different, and the nurseries of countless mother seals are transformed into slaughter-fields, red with the blood of their murdered darlings, slain in their icy cradles. The young seals are born on the ice which the Arctic Current carries past the shores from the fifteenth to the twentieth of February, and until they are two weeks old they are as white as snow and called "harps." When ten days old they begin to change color and become in a short time of a dark brown; and as they grow very rapidly and yield a much finer quality of oil than the old ones, the object of the hunter is to reach them in their babyhood, while yet fed by their mother's milk, and when they are powerless to escape. So rapid is their growth that by the sixteenth of March they are in the best condition to be taken. By the first of April they begin to leave the ice and take to the water, and can be no longer so easily captured. When a vessel reaches an ice-field, where the seals are visible, the men eagerly bound upon the ice, and the work of destruc-

tion begins. These innocent animals are usually
found around a water-hole or along the shore of an
ice-field—hundreds of them, like soldiers in a row,
with their pretty heads extending over the ice anx-
iously looking for their mothers. The hunter man-
ages to get into a position at a point about sixty yards

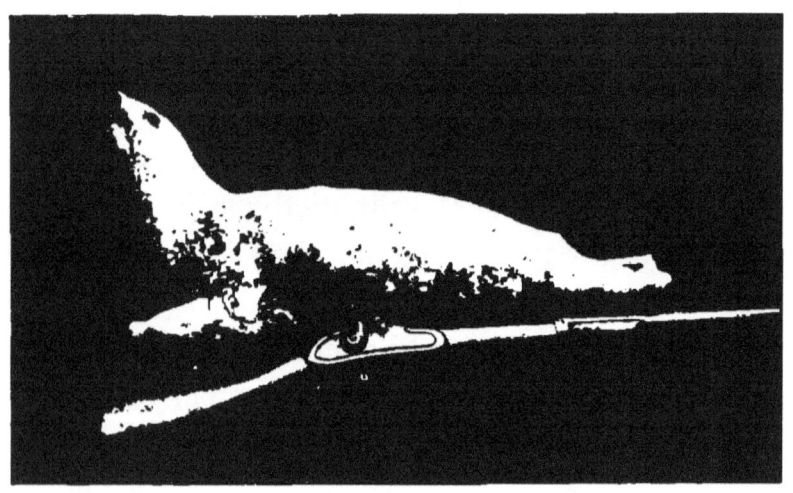

HARP SEAL LESS THAN FOURTEEN DAYS OLD WITH SEALING GUN.

from one end of the line of heads and opens fire with
his great sealing gun; and as these guns are used in
killing reindeer for his winter's meat, a description of
them will be given in another chapter.

As the distance at which this remarkable gun will
do effective work in seal hunting has been forever set-

tled, it is used as a standard among the natives, and should you meet one on land or ice and make inquiry concerning the distance to a certain point the answer would be one, two, three or four "gunshots, sir"—meaning 60, 120, 180 or 240 yards, as the case might be. These guns, loaded with from four to six inches of powder and a handful of about No. 3 buckshot, make a formidable weapon, and as a rule kick backward almost as much as forward; and as they frequently jump overboard into the water when fired from the small boats, it is necessary to have them securely fastened to one end of a stout rope, the other end being attached to the boat, so that the gun can be retrieved after the shot is fired, if it has attempted an escape to the briny deep. Of later years the killing is mostly done with a club, one end of which is armed with a gaff or hook— a light blow on the nose being sufficient to stun the animal. Instantly the scalping knife, which is ever ready in the belt, is brought into use, and in a few moments the carcass is quivering on the ice, stripped of its skin, to which the fat adheres. The pelts are then dragged to the ship over the ice and taken to port, where the skins and fat are separated, the former being salted for exportation, and the latter manufactured into oil at either St. John's or Harbour Grace, where all the seal oil is manufactured.

4

SALMON INDUSTRY.

Nowhere are there any finer salmon streams than those of Newfoundland; but as no proper measures have been taken for their preservation, the average export for the past ten years has scarcely exceeded $100,000.00. Barring the rivers and brooks with nets at the times when the fish are ascending to spawn, constructing weirs, traps and dams, sweeping the pools in the rivers with seine-nets, and night-spearing, have been carried on for generations by ignorant and reckless persons, goaded on by the greed of immediate gain; so that in the streams the salmon are almost exterminated, though in the lakes they are abundant, take the hook well, and in flavor compare favorably with those of any country. There is, however, a prospect that through the efforts of a Fish Commission, which has lately been established, the streams will be opened up and the salmon will return to their old haunts.

HERRING.

Herring are plentiful and of the finest quality; but as the cod is or has been the staple stock in trade, they too have been sadly neglected. Had the herring fishery been prosecuted with as much vigor as the cod, proper care bestowed on the curing and packing, and the whole placed under proper regulations, it might to-day approach the cod fishery in value. The chief seats of herring fishing are Fortune, Placentia, St. George's, and Bay of Islands, and the average annual value is about as follows: Export, $358,359.00; sold to French and Americans for bait, $150,000.00; and allowing 73,000 barrels for home consumption at $3.00 per barrel, gives us a grand total of $727,359.00.

LOBSTER.

According to the last census (1891) there were then 340 lobster factories, employing 4,807 persons. The report of the Department of Fisheries for 1893 states that the total number of lobster traps amounted to 87,720, and that there were caught 5,054,462 lobsters, from which number 26,214 cases of lobsters (each case containing forty-eight one-pound cans) were packed. These returns apply only to licensed factories; besides there were a large number of unlicensed factories on the French shore. The total value from 1888 to 1892, inclusive, was $2,067,408.00.

CHAPTER V.

The Soil Neglected—False Representations as to its Value—
Delay in Development of Interior—The Geological Survey
sets Things Right—Fertile River Valleys—Farm Products
in 1891—Domestic Animals.

EVEN up to a comparatively recent period,
the inhabitants were so busily engaged in
the fishing industry that no attention whatever was paid to the cultivation of the soil, and those
who most profited by the arduous labors of the fishermen, in order to keep them huddled along the rugged
coast, assiduously taught them to regard the interior
of the island as a hopelessly barren waste, unfit for
the occupancy of man. That this is not the case has
been clearly demonstrated by the geological survey.
According to its reports, there are in the valleys on the
weastern coast 1,320 square miles " perfectly capable
of being reclaimed and converted into fairly produc-
tive grazing and arable land," and these valleys are as a

LEADING TICKELS, A SAMPLE COAST TOWN.

rule well wooded.   In the great valleys of the Gander,
Gambo, Terra Nova and Exploits there are 3,320
square miles of land suitable for farming, the soil being of a rich loam, composed of alluvial deposit and decayed vegetable matter.   There are also many smaller
fertile tracts around the heads of bays and lakes, and
along the smaller streams, making in all not less than
5,000 square miles of land suitable for cultivation.
The census of 1891 showed that only 179,215 acres
were actually occupied, as follows: 64,494 acres of improved land, 20,524 acres in pasture, 21,813 acres in
gardens, and 6,244 acres of improved land unoccupied.

FARM PRODUCTS FOR 1891.

The farm products for 1891 are shown by the statistical reports to amount to:

491 bushels wheat, @ $1.00..............	$491
12,900 bushels oats, @ .50	6,450
36,032 tons hay, @ $20.00	720,640
481,024 barrels potatoes, @ $1.00	481,024
60,235 barrels turnips, @ $1.00	60,235
86,411 barrels other roots, @ $1.00.........	86,411
401,716 pounds butter, @ .20	83,343
154,021 pounds wool, @ .20...................	30,804
Milk and vegetables............................	96,000
Total.....................................	$1,562,398

DOMESTIC ANIMALS.

If to this aggregate be added the value of the calves, sheep, swine, horses, goats and fowls raised during the same year, in round numbers $732,000.00, we have a grand total of $2,295,398.00 for the agricultural products of the island for the year 1891. The fact must be taken into consideration that this production has not been from the interior, but from a comparatively narrow belt in close proximity to the coast. It is thus conclusively shown what the agricultural possibilities of this land of "cod-fish and fog" would be, if the fertile valleys of the interior were placed under proper cultivation.

CHAPTER VI.

The First Mines—Geological Distribution of the Copper Ores —Lead Ore—Gypsum and Marbles—Iron Pyrites Mine on Pilley's Island—Asbestos—Coal Areas—Petroleum.

HILE the fisheries, lumber and agricultural products are large and remunerative, the mining resources of the island are destined to eclipse all others in the near future.

THE FIRST MINES.

It was not until 1857, when Mr. Smith McKay first discovered copper near a small fishing hamlet called Tilt Cove, in Notre Dame Bay, that any attention was paid to prospecting for minerals. Here a mine was opened in 1864 under the management of Messrs. C. F. Bennett and McKay. During the next fifteen years Tilt Cove mine yielded over 50,000 tons of copper ore, having a market value of $1,572,154, and nickel ore worth $32,740. This mine to-day employs an average of about 500 miners. In 1875 another copper mine was opened at Bett's Cove, a distance of ten or twelve miles south of Tilt Cove. In four years the quantity of ore exported from it amounted to 122,556 tons, with a value of $2,982,836.00. In 1878 a still richer deposit was opened up at Little Bay, near Bett's Cove. Up to 1879 the total quantity of ores exported from all these mines reached a value of $4,629,889.00, or nearly a million pounds sterling. This placed Newfoundland, though still in its kilts as a mining country, sixth among the copper producing countries of the world.

GEOLOGICAL DISTRIBUTION OF THE COPPER ORES.

The existence of the serpentine rocks in the island is a matter of the utmost importance, as they belong to what in Canadian geology is known as the Quebec Group of the Lower Silurian series, and the middle or Lauzon division of that series. That division, according to Sir William Logan, "is the metalliferous zone of the Lower Silurian in North America, and rich in copper ores, chiefly as interstratified cupriferous slates, and is accompanied by silver, gold, nickel and chromium ores." This Lauzon division is the one which is developed in Newfoundland, and in which all the copper mines are located. The Government Geological Survey's report gives the following truthful estimate of these serpentine mineral-bearing rocks of the island, which is sufficient proof of the existence of inexhaustible bodies of valuable minerals, extending over an area of 5,097 square miles:

Between Hare and Pistolet Bays	230	sq. mi.
North from Bonne Bay	350	"
South from Hare Bay........................	175	"
South from Bonne Bay	150	"
South from Bay of Islands	182	"
Surrounding Notre Dame Bay............	1,400	"
Gander Lake and River Country.........	2,310	"
Bay d'Est River	300	"
Total	5,097	sq. mi.

While these remarks are with special reference to the copper ores it must not be forgotten that in the metalliferous zone just referred to others, such as asbestos, nickel, iron pyrites, lead, and iron ore are found, and give promise of profitable development, to which special reference will be made further on.

LEAD ORE.

Lead ore was first discovered at La Manche, at the northeastern extremity of Placentia Bay, where for several years workings have been carried on. This ore is rich, assaying 82 per cent. of metallic lead, as well as a small percentage of silver.

GYPSUM AND MARBLES.

The Geological Survey's report states that "gypsum is distributed more profusely and in greater volume in the carboniferous districts than in any part of the continent of North America of the same extent." In St. George's Bay and Codroy the bodies of gypsum are immense. Marbles also of every shade of color are found in large quantities on both the eastern and western shores; granite of the first quality, building stones, whetstones, stones suitable for grindstones, limestone, and the finest roofing slate it has been the writer's pleasure to look upon.

IRON PYRITES MINE ON PILLEY'S ISLAND.

Our notes of the mineral resources of Newfoundland would be very deficient were not special reference

SECTION OF THE SETTLEMENT AT PILLEY'S ISLAND PYRITES MINE.

made to this great mine, in whose beautiful little harbor our expedition landed on Sunday, October 14, 1894, on our journey to the White Hills. This mine has been worked for the last ten years, and has been and is at present one of the most valuable in the island. The quality of the pyrites is said to be the finest in the world, containing 52 per cent. of sulphur and 42 per cent. of iron, from which is manufactured the finest steel. The ore is mostly shipped to the United States, where it is used in the manufacture of sulphuric acid, copperas and fertilizers, and the demand is steadily increasing; and as there is another deposit adjoining the present mine, should the latter pinch out, the additional lode would furnish an abundance for years to come. The value of iron pyrites exported to the United States from 1886 to the end of 1893, according to the Customs Report, reaches a total value of $759,451.00. The same report shows an aggregate value of $10,799,086.00 of all minerals exported from the island, from 1864 to the end of 1893.

ASBESTOS.

This valuable mineral has been found amongst the serpentine deposits in many places. It occurs in strings or threads of a fine, silky texture, traversing the masses of serpentine in all directions. On the eastern coast of Port-au-Port, rising out of the sea to a nearly vertical height of 1,800 feet, is a mountain known as Bluff Head. This mountain determines the southern boundary of the serpentine. It was here that asbestos first attracted attention. Bluff Head was long known to the fishermen of the neighborhood as "Cotton Rock," and the Hon. Philip Cleary, of St. John's, was the first to equip a small expedition, four years ago, to engage in the work of prospecting, which resulted in the finding of this valuable substance.

COAL AREAS.

The principal carboniferous region of the country is St. George's Bay, where coal was discovered about fifty years ago by Mr. J. B. Jukes, who was for many years Director of the Irish Geological Survey, and who spent twelve months on the island and found a coal seam three feet in thickness, containing cannel coal of excellent quality, cropping out of the right bank of the Middle Barachois Brook, on the south side of St. George's Bay. His estimate of this small portion of the coal basin of Newfoundland was twenty-five miles wide by ten miles in length. In 1873 another seam was discovered by Mr. J. P. How-

ley, F. G. S., at present Director of the Geological
Survey, on Robinson's Brook, four feet in thickness,
very bituminous coking coal, emitting much gas under
combustion, and burning freely. He also found another seam in the same section, seventeen inches
thick. In 1889 a still more thorough examination
of this coal district was made under the direction of
Mr. Howley. Referring to the report of that year, it
shows that altogether fourteen seams of coal, of a
varying thickness, from a few inches up to six feet,
were uncovered on one small brook; three on another
two miles distant, and four on a third brook, still
farther eastward some two and one-half miles. These
with some smaller ones aggregate a thickness of
twenty-seven feet of coal in the section, which is repeated by being brought to the surface again on the
other side of the synclinal trough. From the above
condensed statement from official facts it will be
readily seen that there is not the possibility of a
doubt that coal is abundant on the island; and further, the reader will be surprised to learn that notwithstanding the presence of these rich and extensive
coal fields, none of them have yet been worked, and
they import from Cape Breton and Prince Edward's
Island all the coal they use at an annual expense
of about $250,000.00.

PETROLEUM.

As was to be expected in presence of all this coal,
indications of petroleum in paying quantity have been
observed, and will be investigated and utilized as soon
as the people recover from the present financial
troubles. The writer, being somewhat familiar with
surface indications of petroleum in the great oil fields
of Pennsylvania, noticed in the White Hills region
strong surface signs, including the presence of the well
known pebble rocks, and has not the least doubt but
it is only a question of time when Newfoundland will
be a coal oil producing county.

CHAPTER VII.

Mode of Government—Constitution—Powers of the Governor
   —The Legislature—The Supreme Court—Central District
   Court—Quarter Sessions—Failure in Administration—
   Commercial and Financial Slavery—A Gloomy View—
   From Boom to Crash—The Outlook—Their Hope and
   Prayer.

EPRESENTATIVE Government was
granted to Newfoundland in 1832. In
1855, after oft-repeated applications by the
people, what is known as "Responsible Government"
was ceded to the colony, which is simply the applica-
tion of the principles of the British constitution to the
island, and provides that the country should be governed according to the well understood wishes of the
people." The party in power, i. e., having the majority in the Legislature, disposes of the principal offices
under the government, and also elects the Executive
Council. The House of Assembly is elected by the
people, and the Legislative Council is nominated by
"the Governor in Council."

CONSTITUTION.

The form of government consists of a Governor who is appointed by the Crown of England, and is paid a salary of $12,000 a year by the Colony; an Executive Council consisting of seven members chosen by the majority in the Legislature, at a salary of $120.00 per session; a Legislative Council of fifteen members, nominated by the Governor in Council and holding office for life at a salary of $120.00 per session; and a House of Assembly at present consisting of thirty-six members, elected by the votes of the people every four years. If they reside in St. John's they receive a salary of $194.00 per session; if resident elsewhere, $291.00. The President receives $240.00 and the Speaker of the House of Assembly receives $1,000.00 per session.

POWERS OF THE GOVERNOR.

The Governor is Commander-in-Chief over the colony, and has the power in the Queen's name to commute sentences of courts of justice; to summon, open, prorogue, and on occasions dissolve the local Parliament; to give or withhold assent to, or reserve for the Royal consideration, all bills which have passed both Chambers.

THE LEGISLATURE.

The Legislature must meet once a year, and is usually summoned "for the dispatch of business" in the month of February.

SUPREME COURT.

A Supreme Court was instituted in 1826 by the promulgation of a Royal Charter. To it and to the magistrates belong the correct interpretation and proper enforcement of the laws. It is composed of a Chief Justice and two Assistant Judges; it holds two terms or sessions each year, on May 20th and November 20th. There are also circuits of the Supreme Court held in the northern, southern and western districts of the island at such times and places as may be fixed by proclamation of the Governor. These are presided over by the Chief Justice or one of the Assistant Judges, in rotation. The yearly salary of the Chief Justice is $5,000.00, and of each Assistant Judge $4,000.00; they hold their appointments for life.

CENTRAL DISTRICT COURT.

The Central District Court is a Court of Records, held in the capital, St. John's, for the adjudication of civil causes, and sits whenever business requires. There are two Judges appointed by the Governor in

5

Council, and a Sheriff for each judicial district, who is also appointed by the Governor.

QUARTER SESSIONS.

Courts of general and quarter sessions are held in such places as may be determined by the proclamation of the Governor, and are presided over by stipendiary magistrates or justices of the peace.

This completes and rounds out the system, which is well enough in form, but as everything depends upon administration, the best forms fail when worked in the interest of others than the governed.

COMMERCIAL AND FINANCIAL SLAVERY.

From the foregoing sketch of the governmental forms, it is easy to see that the enjoyment of even the measure of liberty ostensibly allowed to the people is at the mercy of the administration, and at last of the Crown. The real power is wielded from the other side of the water. How it was used in the past we have already shown; the Newfoundlanders were sheep in the hands of the British shearers. The native or resident population (when at length permitted to reside) caught fish, and their masters took and sold the catch, allowing the fishermen enough to keep them alive. Of course in the world of to-day that could not last among people of Saxon blood; hence reform, relaxation of repressive law, "responsible government." But the situation is changed more in appearance than in reality. Modern methods have changed what was robbery into various forms of swindling. Where a people are thus held in commercial slavery, morality in business and politics will not touch high-water mark; where government is administered with the ulterior object of enriching the few at the expense of the many, it surprises no thoughtful mind that the lesson of example is learned, and those who are preyed upon too often turn to prey upon one another. The recent financial history of Newfoundland is a case in point. Since we came home, in December, 1894, the island experienced a financial cyclone whose wreckage will leave marks for years.

A GLOOMY VIEW.

One of their writers puts it strongly under date of January 30th, 1895: "Newfoundland to-day is a country without banks, without currency, without credit. Its commerce and trade are shattered, its population reduced to hopeless misery." Making due allowance for over-statement natural to too close a view-point, there remains only too much underlying fact. The difficulty about the French fishery rights we have mentioned. France protected her fishermen by a bounty, which drove the Newfoundlanders out of European ports; efforts to secure protection from the home government failed, because it seemed to the British capitalist that his interest lay in putting and keeping the fishermen at the mercy of a few merchants —and there they are, under the "truck system," a relic of ancient barbarism, just a hundred per cent. worse than the "grub stake" of the miners in the United States. The merchants, having skinned the fishermen, are subjected to the same process at the hands of *their* masters; it seems they have been losing money for ten years past, in the vain struggle with French bounty-fed competition. Meanwhile the professional politician comes to the front, fomenting strife between factions while he gnaws all the marrow from the bone of contention. Scarcity of currency added to the difficulty.

FROM BOOM TO CRASH.

The fire that almost destroyed St. John's in 1892 put some five million dollars of insurance and relief funds in circulation, and thus started a "boom" of fictitious prosperity; but this was only superficial, and the crisis, inevitable in such conditions, came in the winter of '94–'95. When the two prominent banks, the Union and Commercial, went to the wall, the exposure was simply amazing. The former had overdrafts aggregating more than two millions, half of it standing against accounts of directors; the latter had overdrawn accounts of the same amount, half to directors, one of whom had $657,000. The combined capital of the two banks was but $800,000. What wonder that the ensuing crash left conditions such as described in our quotation above? Verily, the honest native Newfoundlander, who creates the wealth of the country, has "fallen among thieves!"

THE OUTLOOK.

What will be the outcome? No man knows. The *animus* of those who have the ear of the English capitalists, and through them of the home government, is well shown in the following from the St. John's correspondence of tne New York *World:*

"The widespread ruin and mystery that resulted need not be dwelt upon. Suffice it to say that it crippled the country and beggared its people. The people are now getting themselves together again, the merchants are, to all intents and purposes, swept away, and knowing that they must depend upon themselves in future, the fishermen are preparing to prosecute their industry with the best resources they have got, and we have faith in the ultimate result.

"It became a matter of great difficulty to obtain money to meet the interest on the public debt, due December 31, without meeting which we should have become insolvent. It was finally secured, at a great sacrifice, and then, having breathing space, the Government sought the aid of England to guarantee interest on a loan to complete our railway, which had to be stopped when the crash came.

"She refused to help us, unless we accepted an unconditional Royal Commission. This our Government would not do, fearing we should be made a Crown colony.

"Then we turned to Canada, which has for twenty-five years been tempting us to join the Confederation, and sought terms of admission from her. Unaided she could not assume the whole burden of our public debt, $15,000,000. She would take two-thirds of it, and requested England to assume the remainder. But again England refused and blocked a second avenue of escape for us.

"This compelled us to adopt the last resort and appeal to the liberty-loving and large-hearted people of the United States. Colonial Secretary Bond is now endeavoring to secure a loan there to enable us to tide

over our difficulties. England's enmity is manifest.
She is throwing every obstacle in the way to prevent
our succeeding. Her object is to prevent us from
securing help abroad and so compel us to bankrupt on
June 30, when our next half-yearly interest becomes
due. Then she will revoke our charter of self-govern-
ment and reduce us to a Crown colony."

THEIR HOPE AND PRAYER.

And this in the end of the nineteenth century,
under the electric light, at the hands of the Government of Her Majesty, Victoria the Good! Can it be
wondered at that the islanders are unwilling to trust
the Crown, or even federation into the Dominion, but
look with laying hope for the great Republic to reach
northward and take North America from the St.
Lawrence to Baffin's Bay under the protection of the
Stars and Stripes? This feeling was manifest to us in
the "open sesame" effect of the name of American
wherever it was heard. To be sure we have our
financial crashes and crises, but we have not yet been
reduced to the commercial slavery that has nearly
crushed our island neighbors.

CHAPTER VIII.

EDUCATION.

Academies — Colleges — Pupil Teachers — London University Centre — Jubilee Scholarship — Council of Higher Education.

REVIOUS to the year 1823 no organized attention was paid to education in the colony. The people were poor, and it required a hard struggle for daily bread. The settlements were small, widely separated, and physical wants were too pressing to permit scarcely any attempt at the education of the rising generation, and, as a matter of fact, they grew up without the first rudiments of knowledge outside of their vocation of capturing cod and seal. The beginning of common school education dates from 1823, when "The Newfoundland School Society" was founded in London by Samuel Codner, a Newfoundland merchant. Afterwards its name was changed to "The Colonial and Continental Church Society." The schools it planted were maintained by the liberality of its members unaided until 1843, when the Legislature granted an annual sum of $5,100 for the promotion of common school educa-

tion. In the same year the same body made provision for higher education by establishing an academy in St. John's. This did not succeed, and was abandoned in 1850. In its place three academies were founded, on the denominational principle, and at a later date a fourth was established.

COLLEGES.

These four schools, which are connected respectively with the four different religious denominations, have expanded, and done much toward the education of the people. They are conducted by teachers of ability and character, and give excellent training. At the present time they are known as the Roman Catholic College, Church of England College, Methodist and Presbyterian Colleges respectively. The two last named lost their buildings in the great fire of 1892, but the Methodist buildings have been restored, and are more spacious and better equipped than those destroyed. The Presbyterian College has also been rebuilt, and now occupies its new building.

PUPIL TEACHERS—LONDON UNIVERSITY CENTRE.

The training of teachers is one of the important features of these colleges. They must pass rigid examinations and are graded according to merit before they are permitted to take charge of schools. Students are also prepared for the Universities, and St. John's has been made a centre of the London University, so that pupils can here prepare for and pass the matriculation examinations which admit them to that old and honored institution.

JUBILEE SCHOLARSHIP.

As a futher incentive to those who aspire to higher education, "The Newfoundland Jubilee Scholarship" has been founded. The Governor in Council appropriates an annual sum of $480.00 for the institution of a scholarship in the London University, to be given to the student who shall take the highest percentage among competitors in and from the colony at the matriculation examinations held in June and January of each year.

COUNCIL OF HIGHER EDUCATION.

In 1893 an act was passed "to provide for Higher Education." This act provides for the appointment of a Council to consist of twenty-three members, and makes the Superintendents of Education and Headmasters of Colleges members *ex officio*. The sum of $4,000.00 is appropriated annually to carry out the provisions of the act, and the Jubilee

Scholarship is subject to the regulations of this Council.

The governmental appropriation in 1893 for colleges, grammar and elementary schools, was $151,-891.22. Of this amount the common or elementary schools received $97,753.15; pupil teachers, $5,610.84; encouragement of teachers, $25,297.87; inspectors, $6,060.00.

The number of common schools in 1893 was as follows: Church of England, 194, with an attendance of 11,808; Church of Rome, 200, with an attendance of 10,265; Methodist, 144, with an attendance of 8,465; Presbyterian, Congregational and others 10, with an attendance of 296—making a total of 33,834 pupils attending the common or elementary schools, which, when added to the number of pupils attending the different colleges, makes a grand total of 34,557 pupils attending schools.

CHAPTER IX.

Roads Unknown to Early Settlers—Selfish Policy of Mother
Country—Fences and Chimneys Prohibited—Reform Be-
gins in 1813—First Road in 1825—Road Grant in 1832—
Road Building Leads to Discovery of Minerals—Geological
Survey—Visions of Railways Looming up—Sir William
Whiteway's Scheme—First Railway Contract in 1881—
First Sod Cut—In the Hands of a Receiver—Change of
Government and Railway Extension—Sir William Again
at the Helm—A New Survey—Northern and Western
Railway—Railway Extension Means More Common Roads
—Mails by Railway—Route of Railway—Newfoundland
no Longer an Island.

IN no other country whose discovery dates
back as far as Newfoundland has the material and social advancement of the people
been so seriously retarded by the want of roads. The
original settlement of the island took place entirely in
connection with the fisheries. The gathering of the
abundant and valuable harvest from the tempestuous
sea was the only industry attempted or contemplated.
Around the rock-bound coast, in little secluded coves
and harbors, the fishermen (chiefly from England,

Ireland and Scotland) collected in small hamlets and villages, in such localities as were best adapted for catching, drying and shipping fish. Thus distributed along the coast, they were generally widely separated, and intercourse was maintained mostly by sea, or by rude paths through the woods and rocks between neighboring settlements. Had the clearing and cultivation of the soil been combined with fishing, the construction of roads would have become an absolute necessity; but the selfish policy established by the mother country, at the bidding of the English capitalists who carried on the fisheries, effectively prevented colonization. That policy was to keep the island solely as a fishing station, in order to train seamen for the British navy. All grants of land were prohibited, the cultivation of the soil was made a penal offense, and for a long time a most vigorous attempt was made to make the fishermen migratory by carrying them home at the close of each season to return the following summer. In 1790 one of the Governors publicly announced that he "was directed not to allow any possession as private property to be acknowledged in any land whatever which is not actually employed in fishery." In 1799 Governor Waldegrave ordered fences which had been erected, enclosing a piece of ground, to be torn down, and prohibited chimneys even in the temporary sheds used for sheltering the fishermen. Though the progress of the colony was thus prevented and discouraged in every conceivable manner, the sturdy pioneers held their ground, or rather rocks, on the coast, and increased in numbers until in 1813.

THE DAWN APPEARED.

The foolish, cruel and selfish laws were relaxed, and grants of land to settlers were for the first time permitted. Agriculture, on a small scale, immediately began in close proximity to each settlement. The settlers found in a short time that the argument used by those who were interested in keeping the country unsettled, that the climate and soil were wholly unsuited to agriculture, was a malicious falsehood manufactured out of the whole cloth.

ROAD MAKING BEGINS.

It was soon found that little progress could be made in the cultivation of the soil until roads were constructed. The year 1825 was made memorable by the building of the first road, nine miles in length, from St. John's to Portugal Cove, on the southern shore of Conception Bay. On the opposite shore of this bay were the thriving towns of Harbour Grace,

Carbonear and Brigus, the centres of a considerable population. By establishing a regular system of boats to cross this bay, carrying mails and passengers, a route was established by which nearly half the population in the country were provided with an imperfect means of communication.

To Sir Thomas Cochrane, then Governor, belongs the distinguished honor of introducing this important step in the furtherance of civilization. He also constructed a road to Torbay, a village north of St. John's; and a third along a beautiful valley through which flows a small stream falling into St. John's harbor at a point now known as Waterford Bridge.

This beginning of road making took place only seventy years ago, but the progress made has been most remarkable. Year after year roads radiating from St. John's in various directions were built, along which farms and neat farmhouses soon became visible. One of these roads extends first to Topsail on Conception Bay, thence to Holyrood, at the head of the bay, and further on to Salmonier, St. Mary's and Placentia.

When representative government was established in 1832, an annual grant was voted for making and repairing roads and bridges, and of late years over $150,000 per annum have been expended for this purpose. The Great Northern Mail road for establishing communication with the people of the northern bays was begun and pushed to completion, and at the present writing there are about 1,000 miles of postal roads and 2,000 miles of district roads.

ROAD BUILDING LEADS TO THE DISCOVERY OF MINERALS—A GEOLOGICAL SURVEY.

As road building necessitated surveys into and through the interior, as well as the disturbance of the rock and earth in numerous places, it led to the discovery of minerals, and finally (in 1864) to the establishment of a most efficient Geological Survey. Sir William Logan, the eminent geologist of Canada, was applied to, who nominated Mr. Alexander Murray, who had been his efficient assistant for twenty years, to take charge of the work. He prosecuted it for over twenty years, and it has been continued with commendable zeal by his able assistant, Mr. James Howley, up to the present time.

VISIONS OF RAILWAYS LOOMING UP.

Thus, after being a mere fishing station for 250 years, without farms or roads, the fringe along the coast was intersected with public highways, the cultivation of the soil was making some progress, and many of sturdy "old salts" were making themselves comfortable homes, and while they were braving the billows on the banks and their fish were drying on the flakes, the fertile ground was growing crops. Instead of reaping the harvest from the sea alone, the land also contributed to the support of themselves and little ones, and the one avocation interfered but little with the other.

About this time a proposition was made by Mr. Sanford Fleming, Engineer-in-Chief of Canadian railways, which helped to start the public mind to thinking of the possibility of constructing a railway across the island. He published a paper in which he advocated that the shortest route between America and England was across Newfoundland. He suggested a fast line of steamers from Valentia, Ireland, to St. John's, Newfoundland, carrying only passengers, mails and light express goods. Thence he proposed to build a railway across the island to St. George's Bay, where another swift line of steamers would ply to Shippegan, in the Bay of Chaleur, where connection with American railways would be obtained. He calculated that the ocean passage would not exceed four days, and that passengers from London would reach New York in seven days. So convincing were his arguments that the Newfoundland Legislature appropriated a sum of money for a preliminary survey which was made in 1875 under the direction of Mr. Fleming. Two years then elapsed before any other steps were taken. At length, Sir William Whiteway, Premier of the colony, to whom belongs the honor, of not only introducing the railway system in the face of the most bitter opposition, but of perseveringly carrying it out for more than fourteen years as a prominent feature of his policy—undertook to grapple with the matter in earnest. His first experiment was (following the lines drawn by Mr. Fleming) to offer an annual subsidy of $120,000.00 and liberal land grants along the line to any company that would construct and operate a line across the island, to be connected by steamers with England on the one side, and on the Gulf of St. Lawrence on the other with Canadian railways. The imperial government, however, refused to sanction this policy on the ground that it might be regarded by the French as an infringement of their fishing rights, which were secured by treaty, on the west coast where the terminus would be. This project, therefore, had to be abandoned.

Two more years elapsed, when Sir William conceived the idea of building a narrow-gauge road suited to local requirements, and to be known as the Hall's Bay line. The resolutions which he submitted to the

House of Assembly proposed the construction of a road from St. John's, the capital, to Hall's Bay, the centre of the mining region, with branches to Harbour Grace and Brigus, the total length of which would be about 340 miles. Such a line would open up for settlement the large areas of good lands and valuable timber districts already referred to in the valleys of the Gambo, Terra Nova, Gander and Exploits, and connect the mining region with the capital. A joint committee of both houses of the Legislature was appointed to consider the proposition. Their report concluded by recommending the passage of an act authorizing a loan of the amount required to construct the line, within the limits of one million pounds sterling, and in sums not exceeding half a million of dollars in any one year. This report was adopted by the Legislature by an overwhelming majority. Railway commissioners were appointed and engineers were employed, and during the summer and autumn of 1880 a preliminary survey of the southern portion of the proposed line was made, and this led to the

FIRST RAILWAY CONTRACT IN THE COLONY.

When the Legislature met in 1881 the tender of an American syndicate for building the road was accepted. The leading features of the contract were as follows: A line of narrow-gauge road (3 feet, 6 inches) from St. John's to Hall's Bay, with branches to Brigus and Harbour Grace, a distance estimated at 340 miles; steel rails; a money subsidy of $180,000.00 to be paid half-yearly by the Government for thirty-five years, conditional on the efficient maintenance and operation of the line; and as each five miles are completed and approved, land grants of five thousand acres per mile of good land to be secured to the company in alternate blocks along the line in quantities of one mile in length and eight miles in depth, and if good land could not be obtained along the line it was to be selected elsewhere.

FIRST SOD CUT.

The first sod was turned on August 9th, 1881, and by September, 1882, thirty-five miles were completed and in running order, one hundred miles were located, and the remainder under survey. By November, 1884, the line was completed and open for traffic between St. John's and Harbour Grace, a distance of eighty-three and one-half miles.

IN THE HANDS OF A RECEIVER.

Soon after the Newfoundland Railway Company failed and all work was stopped. The company failed to complete their contract and the line passed into the hands of a receiver on behalf of certain stockholders in England, and under this arrangement it has been satisfactorily operated up to the present time.

CHANGE OF GOVERNMENT AND EXTENSION OF THE RAILWAY.

In 1885 a change of government took place, and Sir Robert Thoburn became Premier. Not discouraged by the failure of his predecessors, he and his colleagues in 1886 began the construction of a branch twenty-seven miles in length, from Whitbourne Junction to Placentia, the old French capital, which they completed and opened in 1886. This brought the inhabitants in and around Placentia Bay not only in touch with each other but with St. John's, the capital, and proved to be a great benefit to the whole southern and western shores of the bay. The locomotive, the great civilizer in all countries, had now gotten such a foothold that it mattered not which of the political factions got the reins of the government, the work of railroad building was sure to proceed.

The up-country people were still clamoring for their section and the northern extension to Hall's Bay, the great mining centre, and seven miles of the Placentia extension were available for this purpose.

The government decided that the line should be built, and, in 1889, the Legislature passed a Railway Extension Act of a liberal character with scarcely a dissenting voice, which pledged the Government to make a survey of the line to Hall's Bay that same year, and to at once begin the construction of the road at a rate of not less than twenty-five miles a year. Before winter set in some fifteen miles of this railroad from Placentia Junction northward were built.

SIR WILLIAM AGAIN AT THE HELM.

At the November election in 1889, the Whiteway-ites again became victorious. Sir William again became Premier, and soon showed that he had lost none of his former confidence in railway extension as a means of developing the varied resources of the colony. In 1890 the Legislature passed an act providing for the extension of the line towards Hall's Bay, with a branch to Brigus at Clarke's Beach, authorizing a loan of $4,500,000.00 and giving the government authority to accept bids and enter into a contract for the construction of the road. Mr. R. C. Reid, of Montreal, Canada, was awarded the contract, and in October, 1890, work was begun, which was to be completed in five years.

A NEW DISCOVERY.

In the meantime a survey was made from the valley of the Exploits to the west coast of the island, or what is known as the "French Shore." This line passed through the valleys of Deer Lake and Harry's Brook. The result was that inasmuch as it passed through large areas of rich loamy soil, and tapped a portion of the fine Humber valley, famous for its good land and fine pine timber, and terminated on the French Shore in the Bay of Islands, with its magnificent scenery, the government was led to abandon the route north to Hall's Bay, and build the road west from the Exploits.

NORTHERN AND WESTERN RAILWAY.

A new contract was made with Mr. Reid, by which he was to "build, construct and equip a line of railway commencing at the terminus of the road to be constructed under the Northern Railway contract, being a point two hundred miles distant from Placentia Junction and running by the most desirable and most direct route to the northeast end of Gander Lake, thence to the northeast end of Deer Lake, and westerly along the north side (afterwards changed to the south side) of Deer Lake, and down the Humber River, thence by the way of north side of Harry's

River, and thence to Port-aux-Basques." This contract was signed by both parties on the 16th day of
May, 1893.

On the same day another contract was entered into
with Mr. Reid to operate for ten years the Placentia
branch railway and also the "Newfoundland Northern and Western," as the new line from Placentia
Junction to Port-aux-Basques was to be called. This
contract was quite full and strict; among the many
provisions included were a sum of $15,600.00 per
mile; fee simple land grants as follows: 250,000 acres
upon completion of the northern line to Exploits, 250,-
000 acres upon completion of the line to Port-aux-
Basques, and the balance at the completion; land to
be located on each side of the road, and in alternate
sections of one or two miles in length and eight
miles deep; and one commendable section of the
contract stipulates that the daily wages of laborers
shall not be less than one dollar a day, and payable
monthly.

In October, 1890, as per contract, the work was begun with vigor; at the close of 1891 sixty-five miles
were completed and operated, and by the fall of 1893
two hundred miles were completed and trains were
running between Exploits, Whitbourne and St.
John's.

EXTENSION OF RAILWAY NECESSITATES ADDITIONAL COMMON ROADS.

In order to connect the settlements on the seacoast with the railroad, the public highways became a necessity, and these have been mostly surveyed and built by the contractor, Mr. Reid, acting under governmental supervision. A good wagon road forty miles in length has been built from Trinity to Shoal Harbor via Goose Bay, opening up a large area of good land suitable for grazing and agricultural purposes, and furnishes access to railway facilities for a considerable population. Another road ten miles in length connects with Indian Arm Bay; while a third five miles in length runs from Alexander Bay to the railroad near Gambo, and one about forty-four miles long from Hall's Bay, connecting four miles west of Badger Brook. Roads from Arnold's Cove and Come-by-Chance have also been completed.

MAILS BY RAILWAY.

The railway now carries nearly all the northern mails, which in winter used to be conveyed by couriers on foot, or with the aid of dogs over the ice and snow. Small steamers ply from Shoal Harbor, Exploits and Clode Sound around the bays, carrying mail and passengers to and from the various settlements; and thus both social and material progress has been initiated by the iron horse and his satellites, the common roads.

ROUTE OF RAILWAY.

From Placentia Junction, seven miles from Whitbourne, the new line runs northerly, crossing the isthmus which connects the Peninsula of Avalon with the main body of the island, at its narrowest point being only three miles wide. On either side of the isthmus are the heads of the two great bays of Placentia and Trinity. Still following a northerly course, the road passes through Terra Nova, Gambo and Gander Valleys, and enters the valley of the Exploits at Norris' Arm. From this point it turns westerly, following up the Exploits valley and crossing the river at Bishop's Falls, ten miles from its mouth, on a magnificent steel bridge, 630 feet in length, with granite piers and abutments. From Bishop's Falls it crosses over into the valley of the Peter's Arm Brook (the Grand Falls being about one and one-half miles from the road at the two hundred and twenty-second mile from Whitbourne), but returns to the Exploits valley again near Rusby Pond at the two hundred and twenty-seventh mile from Whitbourne. From thence it follows up the Exploits valley to Badger Brook, where it leaves the river. From Badger Brook it takes a northwesterly route, crossing the White Hill Plains, thence down the valley of Kitty's Brook to the northeastern end of Grand Lake. The course is then along the southern side of Deer Lake to Bay of Islands, thence through the valley of Harry's Brook to Bay St. George. From this point the line passes back of the Anguille range of hills, down the valley of the Codroy River to Cape Ray, about nine miles distant from Port-aux-Basques, which is the terminus of the line. When this road is completed it will be five hundred and fifty miles in length, from St. John's on the east coast to Port-aux-Basque on the west, and from the latter point a short sail across the Gulf of St. Lawrence will land passengers on the continental railway system, and Newfoundland will almost cease to be an island.

CHAPTER X.

THE ABORIGINES.

Beothiks or "Red Indians"—Their Condition when Discovered—A Powerful and Warlike People—A Change Comes Over their Dreams—Their Decadence—The Race Extinct—A Melancholy Find—The First White Men to Sight Newfoundland—White Men Land on the Island—From Eighteen to over Two Hundred Thousand.

WHEN the question is asked, who were the first inhabitants of the island of Newfoundland,—to what race of men did they belong, what were their appearance and habits, their color and modes of living?—the sages of the world are not prepared to answer. Recorded history enables us to go back only to the first appearance of European explorers some four hundred years ago, but it is barely possible that other races may have preceded the

"RED INDIANS" OR BEOTHIKS,

Who were the occupants of the soil when the daring voyagers braved the tempestuous Atlantic in their frail crafts, and after untold hardships reached the seagirt isle, and found it inhabited by a race in all respects resembling the savage tribes of the North American continent, and likely belonging to the same stock. The early explorers, thinking they had discovered the eastern shores of Asia or India, called all the inhabitants, both in North and South America, "Indians," and from their complexion the northern tribes were afterwards called "Red Indians."

The race found in Newfoundland called themselves "Beothiks," which was their tribal name. Their features were those of the continental Indians. They had straight, jet-black hair, high cheek bones, small black eyes, and their skin was copper colored. Their habits of life were also similar in many respects; they subsisted by hunting and fishing; their weapons, wigwams and domestic utensils resembled those of neighboring tribes. Among learned men who have carefully studied the few relics which have been preserved, and the meagre and uncertain vocabularies which contain all that remains of their language, there is a difference of opinion as to whether they were a branch of the widespread and warlike Algonquins, who sustained themselves and increased in numbers.

CONDITION OF THE BEOTHIKS WHEN DISCOVERED.

When Cabot landed on the island, in 1497, the Beothiks were a numerous and powerful people, well developed physically, ingenious, of quick intelligence, gentle in manners, and inclined to be friendly to the pale-faces. The great island, with its abundance of wild creatures of many species, and its shores, lakes and rivers swarming with fish, was to them a perfect paradise. Countless herds of reindeer wandered over the marshes in the interior in their migrations, at which times their capture was easily accomplished, even with the simple devices in the possession of these children of the forest. The flesh furnished them with their most nutritious food, while from their pelts they made the best waterproof leather, with which they clothed their feet as well as covered their wigwams, insuring them against the severity of the long winters. These hides, being better adapted for making "buckskin," than those of any other of the deer family, together with the skins of the beaver, wolf and bear, gave them abundant and comfortable clothing. They practiced no agriculture, but the wild berries in their luxuriant growth supplied them with an abundance of vegetable food.

A CHANGE COMES OVER THE DREAMS OF THE BEOTHIKS

That very ancient principle in nature's laws of the survival of the fittest came in force with the appearance of the white man and sealed their doom. For three hundred years they struggled on, but gradually becoming weaker and weaker. For a comparatively short time the same old story repeated itself, and friendly relations existed between them and the invaders; but soon quarrels arose, and deeds of violence resulted in savage vengeance. The first rude trappers, hunters and fishermen as they spread into the northern parts of the island were beyond the control of law and justice, and little disposed to exercise conciliation and kindness towards the untutored savages, whose presence interfered with their pursuits. The poor Beothiks were treated with cruel brutality, and for long years were regarded as vermin to be hunted down and destroyed without limit, except as to opportunity. This led the Indians to fierce, savage retaliation which ensured their ultimate destruction.

THE RACE EXTINCT.

At length the spirit of humanity roused from its deep slumber, and from 1760 to 1823 attempts were made to conciliate the Indians and save their wretched remnant from annihilation; but these efforts proved to have begun too late. Sad experience led them to distrust and hate the white man, and they could not respond to approaches of kindness;

Forlorn and in despair, the few remaining Beothiks
retreated to their last refuge at Red Indian Lake, and
there they died one by one, until not a single living
representative of this once powerful race remained.
There is no darker page in the history of North
America than that which records the fate of the un-
happy Beothiks.

A MELANCHOLY FIND.

In 1828 a final effort was made to open communication with the remnant of the tribe which was supposed to still survive. An expedition was organized
which penetrated to their last retreat at Red Indian
Lake. Only their graves and the mouldering remains of their wigwams were found—but no living
Beothik. The silence of death reigned supreme.
Fragments of canoes, skin dresses, storehouses, and
the repositories of their dead were there, but no
human sound was heard, no smoke from wigwam
seen. Their campfires were extinguished, and the
sad record of an extinct race was closed forever.

THE FIRST WHITE MEN TO SIGHT NEWFOUNDLAND.

Before closing these brief notes of the early history
of this country, it might be well to note the fact that
it is highly probable that the first white men who

saw the shores of Newfoundland were the Northmen. Five hundred years before the time of Cabot these bold adventurers, led by Lief, son of Eric the Red, sailed from Greenland in search of western lands. Newfoundland lay directly in their course, and according to their sagas or books on reaching it they gave it the name of "Helluland," or the land of naked rocks. The daring sailors passed on, however, and made no attempt at forming a settlement. Their adventurous voyage, in which they are said to have reached Rhode Island, took place in 1001.

WHITE MEN LAND ON THE ISLAND.

On the second day of May, 1497, a small caravel named the "Matthew," manned by eighteen English sailors and commanded by John Cabot, left the port of Bristol. Cabot was a Venetian by birth and in the service of Henry VII. of England.

On the twenty-fourth day of June following, hearty English cheers greeted the first sight of the Island of Newfoundland. Thus by right of discovery it belonged to England; but it was not until 1583 that the formal possession was taken by Sir Humphrey Gilbert in the name of Queen Elizabeth. This gallant English knight had formed the purpose of colonizing the island; but misfortunes overtook him, and when re-

7

turning to England his vessel the "Golden Hind" and all on board sunk beneath the waves of the Atlantic.

With these few observations, noting but here and there a few of the most important events in the history of this remarkable island, for many of which we acknowledge indebtedness to that interesting little work by Rev. M. Harvey, of St. John's, entitled "Newfoundland as it is in 1894," the author has hoped to furnish the reader with an outline of the discovery, surface conditions and struggles of the white population of the Hind's crew to a population at present of over two hundred thousand.

CHAPTER XI.

ITH so much knowledge of the history and
physical features of the island as we have
tried to give in the preceding pages, the
reader who has followed us thus far is prepared to accompany us "in the spirit and understanding" as we
now pass to the detailed account of our own personal
experience in hunting the reindeer among the White
Hills of Newfoundland. To the hunter who may follow in our footsteps—and we hope he will be numerous—the space devoted to

PREPARATIONS FOR THE TRIP

May be both interesting and useful; while the tour-
ist will find something of value, and even the stay-at-

home reader should not consider the time altogether wasted which is given to informing him how the "outers" make themselves fairly comfortable under circumstances too commonly described by the opprobrious name of hardship. If some be tempted by our description to "try it on," our work will not have been done in vain.

None of our fellow-sportsmen know better than those who have made frequent excursions to distant fields, how much of a task it is to complete the itinerary; and especially so when the objective point is thousands of miles away, and in a country about whose history the world at large knows but little, and the United States even less. Many letters of inquiry had to be written, and the difficulty was to find the names and addresses of the proper persons with whom to communicate. Fortunately the author noticed a communication from the pen of Wakeman Holbertson which appeared in the April number of Harper's Weekly, 1892, which read like a fairy tale, describing a trip to the White Hills in Newfoundland. The Weekly was passed round, read aloud at a smoke, and commented on to the fullest extent; and while the reputation of Mr. Holbertson for "truth and veracity" was not called into question as a special order of business, the grimaces made by some of the hearers as

Holbertson's story fell upon their ears would have led most observers to conclude that the narrative was a good one, but it had entirely too many caribou in it. It was decided, however, that Mr. A. C. Kepler, with whom the writer has shared elbow-room and blanket on many a hunt in the wilds during the last twenty years, should write Mr. Holbertson for special information. This was promptly done, and in due course of time a reply came verifying all contained in the article and adding still more to it, with a pressing invitation to call and see his trophies of the hunt. It was not long before friend Kepler ostensibly had business in New York, but it is supposed that the business part of that trip was to see Holbertson's heads and horns.

OUR FRIEND'S PUPILS DILATED.

Kepler came back, his pupils as large as a cat's on a dark night, in the dark of the moon, and chattering like a magpie. The whole story was confirmed, and the fall of 1894 was decided upon as the time when our pilgrimage was to be made. So the preliminaries were arranged, and the first step assigned the writer was to open communication with the guide so highly recommended by Mr. Holbertson, whose address we give in large type:

RICHARD LeBUFFE,

HALL'S BAY, P. O. WOLF COVE, NOTRE DAME BAY,

N. F.

No time was lost in addressing a letter containing many questions, and engaging his services for the opening of the season of 1894. After weary weeks of waiting, a letter came bearing the picture of a seal on the stamp, post-marked, "Hall's Bay, Newfoundland." It was short but sweet, and while it did not contain all the information asked, he accepted service on the following terms: Self and canoes, $3.00 per day; four carriers at $1.50 per day each and found; instructions to land at Pilley's Island; charter steam launch to head of Hall's Bay, where guide lives (25 miles); march three miles to foot of West Pond; from foot of pond to head of same, five miles in canoes; march thirteen miles more or less to log tilt on Big Marsh in the White Hills country—in all forty-six miles or more from Pilley's Island to main camp.

Further correspondence elicited the fact that the tilt was constructed of logs chinked with moss, sloping roof of birch bark and a smoke hole, and no way of getting a stove nearer than the head of Hall's Bay, except by carrying it on the backs of men.

All this information suggested the importance of economizing in both weight and bulk, in both personal baggage and supplies. LeBuffe could furnish nothing but his service, that of native carriers, canoes, the log tilt, and all the caribou, ptarmigan and fish our hearts could wish for.

We were also informed that for a party of three or four men four carriers would be required, one of whom would, in addition to packing a good load in and out, act as cook for the party while in camp. From past experience we had learned that if we were

THE CREE STOVE, WHICH, AS IMPROVED, MAKES THE BEST CAMP
STOVE KNOWN.

to be assured of any comfort in camp it would be necessary to take a stove with us, as we had played the smoke-hole racket on many occasions and were not particularly partial to it.

The writer was the possessor of a D. W. Cree camp stove, manufactured in Griggsville, Ills. No better camp stove has been devised; but the one on hand had a cast-iron top, and was both too heavy and too long to be packed on the back of a man. Permission was obtained from Mr. Cree, who is a gentleman sportsman, to have made by our local mechanics a stove after his pattern with modifications to suit our wants. The result was just what we wanted, and the stove proved to be a great comfort as a substitute for the smoke-hole in the log tilt on the Big Marsh. It was twenty-six inches long, thirteen inches high and thirteen inches wide, and made of Russian sheet-iron; top of same material, with two holes covered with sheet-iron lids, in the centre of which was a loose ring. Fire door of the same kind and at the same place as in the Cree stove; the oven, instead of being permanently fixed in position, slid into place on two strong angle-irons, and when not in use could be removed at will, when wood twenty-four inches long could be used. Nine twelve-inch-long joints of galvanized iron telescope pipe, with damper, completed the lightest and best stove of the kind ever used, as far as the writer has been able to ascertain. Weight, with the nine feet of pipe, bake-pan, lids, pipe-collar and baker packed inside, but sixteen pounds. In addition to the stove adjustments it contained when packed for the trip the following

COOKING UTENSILS AND SUNDRIES:

1 coffee pot, ½ dozen tin plates, 1 wire broiler, 2 frying

pans, 2 frying pan handles, 1 large spoon, 1 large meat fork, ½ dozen teaspoons, ½ dozen knives, ½ dozen forks, 1 salt box, 1 pepper box, ½ dozen nested tin cups, 5 oblong nested stew kettles, 1 wash basin, 1 rubber collapsible water bucket, 5 stew kettle lids, 1 butcher knife, 1 dishcloth, 1 cake home-made soap, 2 tea towels.

And, in addition, the following: 1 coil copper wire, assorted wire nails, ½ pound arsenic, 1 pair moccasins, 2 pairs shoe packs, 1 pair heavy woolen stockings, 40 rounds rifle cartridges (40–65), 1 bag chewing tobacco, 2 bags smoking tobacco, 1 pound pulverized alum, and 1 hank heavy cord.

The stove being full, it was padded over the open bottom with excelsior three inches thick for protection to carrier's back, then entirely covered with thick bagging, which was well sewed on and the package completed by buckling on the carrying strap (see cut, page 98), the whole weighing seventy-six pounds—a convenient load for a native Newfoundlander.

BAGGAGE RESTRICTIONS.

Each member of the party was allowed to take as much baggage as he desired to the point of disembarcation, Pilley's Island. When the outfit left Pilley's, each was restricted to the following, a list of which

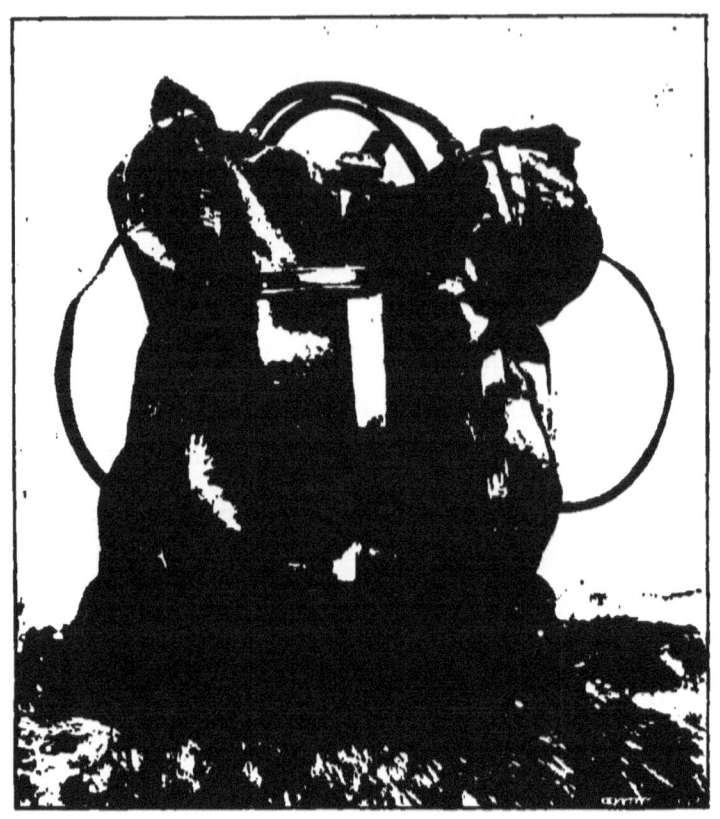

CARRY-ALL WITH CARRYING STRAP ATTACHED.

was sent him : 1 hunting hat, 1 hunting cap, 1 hunting coat, 1 hunting vest, 1 Cardigan jacket, 2 under-
shirts, 2 pairs drawers, 1 pair hunting pants, 1 extra
pair pants, 4 pairs stockings, 2 overshirts, 1 pair hunting shoes, 1 extra pair shoes, 1 pair rubber boots, 1
pair gloves, 1 pair woolen blankets (single), 1 rubber
blanket, 1 carry-all, 1 match safe, ½ dozen handker-

chiefs, 1 towel, 1 washrag, 1 cake toilet soap, 1 gun (rifle or rifle and shot), 1 jointed cleaning rod and oil, 1 light reel, 1 short trunk rod, 1 small fly book, extra hooks, etc., 1 case needles, thread, buttons, 1 compass, 1 hunting knife, 1 rubber collapsible drinking cup, 1 pair slippers (heavy soles), 1 package paper, envelopes, postals, pipes and tobacco, cigars, etc., and one good field or opera grass.

In addition to the above the writer took in a "Ditty Bag" made from an ordinary shot bag the following medical supplies; sufficient for the whole party: 25 sugar coated imp'd. co. cath. pills, 50 sugar coated 2 gr. quin. pills, 50 $\frac{1}{8}$ gr. morph. granules, $\frac{1}{2}$ oz. Norwood's Tr. Verat. Viridi, 2 oz. chloroform, $\frac{1}{2}$ oz. fld. ext. Ipecac, $\frac{1}{2}$ oz. Tr. Dover's powder, 1 oz. oxide zinc ointment, 1 roll rubber adhesive plaster 1 in. wide, 2 drachms stearate of zinc, 3 roller bandages, 1 hypodermic syringe, $\frac{1}{2}$ oz. chlor. anodyne (Parke, Davis & Co.).

Any physician will furnish specific directions for the use of the above named remedies and appliances, in case there is none in the party. The list given embraces all that will be necessary, and the remedies, if handled with a moderate amount of care and intelligence, will meet most of the ills incident to camp life in a northern climate. To this extra personal baggage was added the author's case of

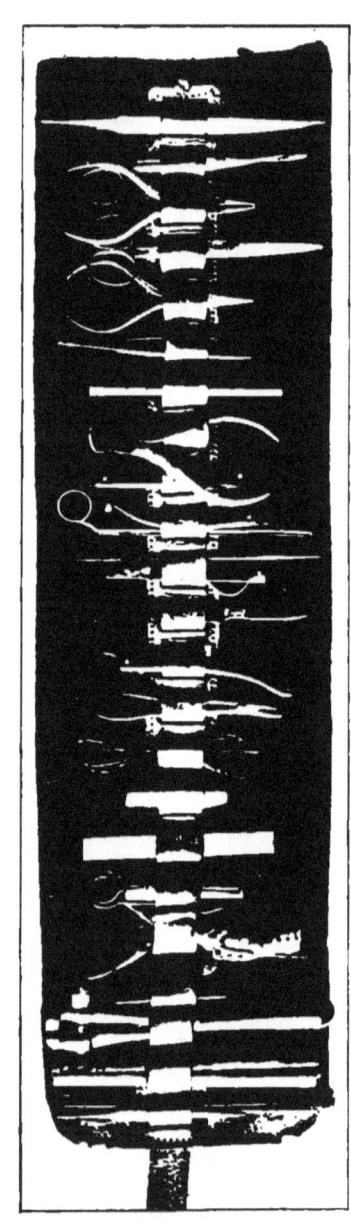

CASE OF CAMP CONVENIENCES USED BY THE AUTHOR IN PREPARING SKINS FOR MOUNTING
AND REPAIRING GUNS AND FISHING TACKLE.

CAMP CONVENIENCES,

which he has for years taken with him, and now deems almost indispensable on fishing, hunting and collecting tours.

GUNS AND AMMUNITION.

As there are still "many men of many minds," it would be impossible to restrict any sportsman as to what arm among the many he should use. Now-a-days there are no poor guns made, comparatively speaking. No man should take two guns into this country unless he can take two in one. He will find that with one and his pack, a tramp of some sixteen miles will give him all he cares to carry. A shotgun is of no earthly use in caribou hunting—you might just as well shoot into a sand-bank. Their covering of short thick hair on a thick hide is almost proof against buckshot. On the other hand the beautiful ptarmigan or willow-grouse are plentiful, of superb flavor, and serve as an agreeable change in diet; but it requires a shotgun to get them. The conditions thus stated suggest the proper gun—either a Daily three-barrel or a gun suggested by the writer, invented and patented by Prof. Wm. B. Hall, of Lancaster, Pa. This gun weighs but eight and one-fourth pounds, and meets all the requirements of any hunt, after any

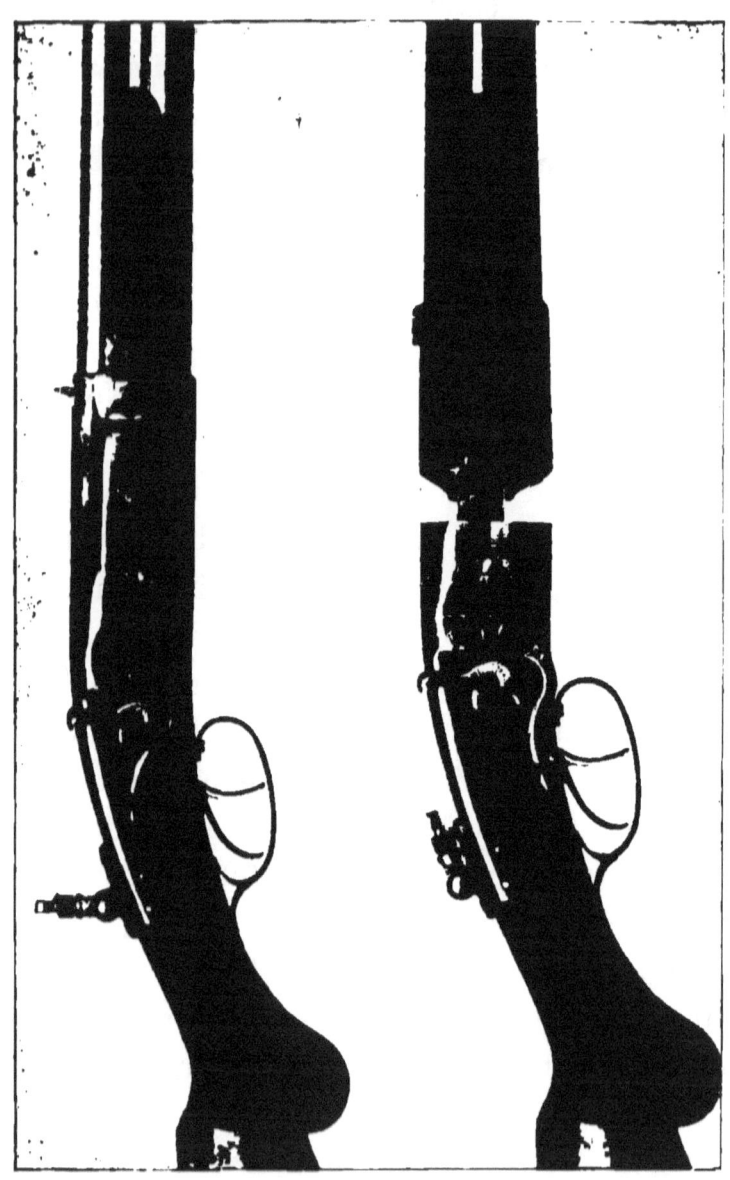

THE HALL COMBINATION RIFLE AND SHOTGUN.

game. The rifle barrel, which is on top, may be made to any calibre to suit the fancy of the owner, from 50 down. The action is strong and perfect. The shot-barrel is a 20-bore cylinder, shoots shot well, and does good execution with a patched round ball at seventy-five to one hundred yards. This would be the ideal gun with jacketed bullet for rifle and smokeless powder. A repeater is not necessary except in war. As each hunter is allowed to kill but five bull and three doe caribou, he should shoot for fine specimens. On small game there is no restriction. As lead is heavy, it is well to take only what ordnance stores are necessary. Forty rounds of rifle cartridges are plenty—and, if a shot-barrel is used, 50 assorted sizes of small shot is quite sufficient. Mr. Kepler carred his Daily 3-barrel gun—the one he has been using for the last fifteen years; shot-barrel 12-bore; rifle, 45–70 Govt. Mr. J. W. Davis, "The Kid" owned no gun, and used the author's Hall gun, 20-bore shot, rifle 40–82. The writer used a 40–65 Winchester with a Malcolm telescope sight.

A small, light tent is a necessity. Having examined carefully the Protean tent, manufactured by A. S. Comstock, of Evanston, Ills., we were not long in selecting just what we wanted. Size, on ground, 7x7 feet; height of rear wall, 2 feet; height at the only pole used, 7 feet 3 inches; 8-ounce army duck. This tent gives more room and stands more blow than any tent made, and the price is reasonable.

Our preparations at this end of the line were now about completed, and in the next chapter we will reach Newfoundland.

THE COMSTOCK ONE-POLE PROTEAN TENT.

CHAPTER XII.

How to Get to Newfoundland—Red Cross Line—The Silvia
and Portia—Time Table and Rates of Fare—No Duty and
Twenty Cubic Feet for Baggage—Marching Orders—Mistake No. 1—On Board the Portia—Off to the North—
Halifax—Fog off Cape Race—Away to St. John's.

HILE the preparations detailed in the last
chapter were being made, the route and
dates were also being arranged. Communication had been established with Messrs. Bowring &
Archibald, Produce Exchange Annex, 9 Stone St.,
New York, who are agents for the *Red Cross Line* of
steamers plying between New York, Halifax, N. S.,
St. John's and Pilley's Island. These two steamers,

THE SILVIA AND PORTIA,

were built especially for this trade, are of high speed,
and have all the modern improvements. One of
them leaves Robinson's, Congress St., Stores Dock,
Brooklyn, fortnightly, sails through Long Island,
Vineyard and Nantucket Sounds, thereby insuring
smooth water, except during a storm, for nearly half

the distance to and from Halifax, which is the first call. The next landing is made at St. John's, Newfoundland. From St. John's they proceed to the Pyrites mines at Pilley's Island, Bay of Notre Dame, 240 miles north of St. John's, and your proper place to stop if you are desirous of securing some fine heads of the North American Reindeer or Woodland Caribou. The

AVERAGE TIME EN ROUTE

northward is as follows:

New York to Halifax............................50 hours.
Stay at Halifax about...........................20 hours.
Halifax to St. John's ....50 hours.
Stay at St. John's................................2 days.
St. John's to Pilley's Island ....24 hours.

And returning southward:

Pilley's Island to St. John's....................24 hours.
Stay at St. John's................................24 hours.
St. John's to Halifax ....50 hours.
Stay at Halifax.............. ....24 hours.
Halifax to New York...........................50 hours.

RATES OF PASSAGE.

The rates here given include meals and state-room berth as well as meals during stops:

Cabin, First Class.

New York to Halifax and return..........................$28.00

New York to St. John's and return 34.00

New York to Pilley's Island and return 72.00

If there are four in the party the accommodating agents will allow an agent's commission of five per cent., which will add $14.40 towards the purchase of provisions for the outfit.

NO DUTY AND TWENTY CUBIC FEET SPACE ALLOWED FOR BAGGAGE.

There is no duty on guns or any other baggage, providing you bring the articles back to the United States; and each passenger is allowed twenty cubic feet of space for baggage, irrespective of weight. Hand baggage and guns are allowed in state rooms.

All preliminaries having been attended to, all we required was a telegram from Bowring & Archibald announcing the arrival and sailing of the *Portia*, which, as we had been informed, would not sail through to Pilley's Island, but connect at St. John's with the coast steamers sailing north, and land us at Pilley's Island about the 12th to the 15th of October.

MARCHING ORDERS.

September 28th, in the early morning, the word came, "*Portia* sails from Robinson's, Congress Street,

Stores, Brooklyn, at 12 M., September 29th." At
4:45 P. M. we boarded the train at Lancaster, Pa.,
with only one incident to mar the pleasant anticipa-
tions which we had been nursing for a year and
more—the one unpleasant thing which occurs on
very many occasions just at the critical moment—
Mr. H. W. Bush, a good hunter and jovial compan-
ion, was obliged to remain at home on account of
business complications over which he had no control.

This sudden break left but three in our party—the
writer, Mr. A. C. Kepler, of Lancaster, and Mr. J. W.
Davis, of Burlington, N. J. This not only deprived
us of the company of Mr. Bush, but as well his share
of the expenses, which amounted to considerable.

The Burlington contingent met us at the Astor
House on Saturday morning, the 29th, as per previous arrangement, and by 10 A. M. we were at the
office of Bowring & Archibald, and soon secured our
passage and each a draft for $100.00 (at an expense of
fifty cents per hundred), as we had already learned
that in Newfoundland American money would be
subject to a shave of three per cent. In this transac-
tion we made a mistake, and others would do well to
benefit by our experience. We should have converted all our money into drafts from $10.00 up,
which would not only have saved us quite a snug

little sum, but would have spared us the mortification of seeing our good United States money discounted by a bankrupt country.

ON BOARD THE PORTIA.

By 11 A. M. we were all on board, had good rooms assigned us, made the acquaintance of the officers and a tour of general inspection. The *Portia* is a fine English steamer of 732 tons, 250 feet long, with accommodations for ninety passengers and a large amount of freight. She is well furnished, kept clean and neat, and the state rooms are large and well arranged. We soon learned that we would not get off at 12 M. As a matter of fact we did not sail until 6 P. M. At 2 P. M. we had a sumptuous dinner, including the delicacies of the season—the sunbrowned veteran, Captain Ash, presiding. He, it will be remembered, was ice-pilot on the *Bear* on the expedition which was sent to Lieut. Greely's rescue. For a quarter of a century he has skirted the ragged ice-bound coasts of Newfoundland, Labrador and Greenland.

OFF TO THE NORTH.

At 6 P. M. the anchor was raised and the *Portia* floated off like a swan. The weather was warm and sultry, and not a cloud in sight as large as a hand.

We all enjoyed the evening sail to the fullest extent and retired at eleven, sleeping soundly until about four on Sunday morning, when we were aroused from our peaceful slumbers by a terrible commotion on deck. The ship was rolling and pitching to such an extent that it was difficult to keep from being thrown from our berths, and the cuspidor was shooting from one side of the room to the other like a billiard ball. In short, we were in a gale. The deck space was mostly taken up by pork, coal oil, apples and other barreled goods, and they were performing the same gyrations as the cuspidors in the state rooms below. At 7 A. M., when opposite Johnstone's Island, the captain wisely concluded to cast anchor and lash the deck load to the railing. At 7 P. M. the anchor was again hauled up and we steamed off, making about six miles, when old Neptune became so boisterous that at one time ten feet of water swept over the *Portia's* forward deck, compelling us to face about again and cast anchor near the spot we had recently left.

Monday, October 1st was cold and clear, though windy. At 5 A. M. we were again under way, rolling along at a fair speed. Though we had but little wind during the afternoon the sea was still rough following the storm, which as will be remembered was very disastrous along the whole Atlantic coast.

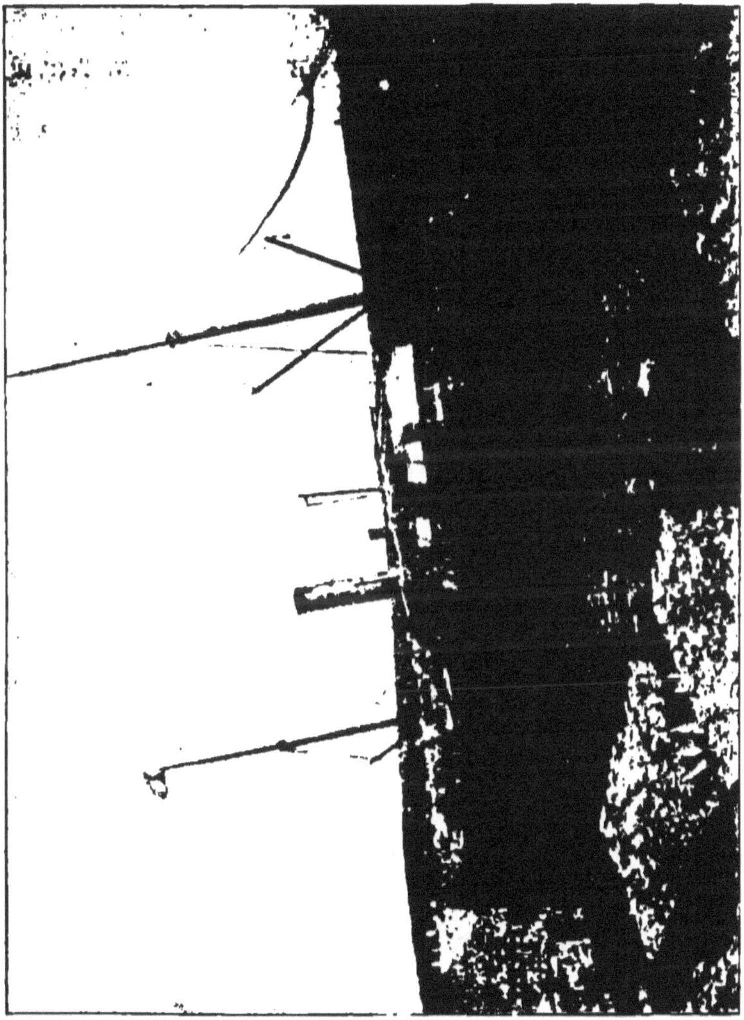

S. S. PORTIA AT HER DOCK, HALIFAX, N. S.

Tuesday, October 2d. Thermometer 56; no wind, clear.

Wednesday, October 3d. Thermometer 50; clear, no wind. We entered the harbor of Halifax, Nova Scotia, at 8 A. M.

HALIFAX.

The city is located in one of the finest harbors in the world, on the Atlantic coast. It forms a loop, the harbor and city being surrounded by high mountains and hills, all sides of which are lined with forts studded with bristling cannon. The first thing we did was to find the post and telegraph offices, after which we made a tour of the city, which is indeed very beautiful, containing massive buildings, fine stores, pretty streets, botanical gardens, museums, etc. We had ample time to walk through all the principal parts of the city, and among the objects of interest we visited the citadel, the most important fort, from which we were afforded a magnificent bird's-eye view of the city and harbor. One of the attractions in the latter was Her Majesty's steamship, the *Blake.* Our paper currency was all right and taken at par, but our silver they refused to take at all. We left Halifax at 3.45 P. M.

Thursday, October 4th. Thermometer 60; cloudy. Began raining this evening, and continued most of the night.

IN A FOG OFF CAPE RACE.

Friday, October 5th. Thermometer 56; fog. At 5.30 this morning we were awakened by the fog signal, which was continued all day, as well as soundings every half hour until we passed Cape Race, when towards evening the fog lifted, and we were running at full speed for St. John's.

CHAPTER XIII.

THE CAPITAL AND ITS SIGHTS.

At St. John's—The Stars and Stripes Raised on our Hotel—A
Hospitable City—Mistake No. 2—Game Laws of Newfoundland—The Stipendiary Magistrate—The License—
Purchasing Supplies—Eight Men for Twenty Days—Two
Dollars a Day " Dry "—Packing for Caché—Mistake No.
3—Rubber the Only Wear—Seeing the City—The Narrows—A Land Locked Harbor—The City—Relative Dis-
tances—The Museum—The Cathedral—Parliament House
—Quidi Vidi.

ATURDAY, *October 6th.* Thermometer 55;
clear. At 4 A. M. we were awakened by
the casting of the anchor in the harbor of
St. John's. We rose at six, collected our hand baggage, passed the customs officers all right, and after a
few minutes' walk up grade we were registered at the
City Hotel, Mrs. G. Walch, proprietress; rate, $1.50
per day, good rooms, comfortable beds, electric light,
bath and plenty of clean, well-cooked, wholesome food.

UP GOES THE STARS AND STRIPES.

Scarcely had the ink time to dry on the register,
when up went the flag of our country in our honor.

We soon learned that the knowledge that one is an American is a sufficient passport in Newfoundland, not only in the capital of the country, but in every hamlet throughout the entire island. Never in any country where it has been the writer's privilege to travel has he been the recipient of so much unsolicited hospitality as was accorded our party during our short stay in St. John's. To mention the names of all who were active in their zeal to make us comfortable and supply us with such information as we desired would be impossible, and to refer to a few would be injustice to all others with whom we came in contact.

After breakfast we started out to attend the business of the hour, and as the sailing date of the first coast steamer north for Pilley's Island governed our stay in St. Sohn's, it was to ascertain of that fact first; so we proceeded to the office of the N. F. Coastal Steamship Company's office, Harvey & Co., where we were informed that the next vessel, the *Virginia Lake*, would sail for Pilley's Island between the 9th and 12th of October. This bit of information also reminded us of

MISTAKE NO. 2,

as we were now to spend at least five or six days in St. John's, at an actual expense of $1.50 a day each, which could all have been saved had we but waited for the *Silvia,* which calls long enough at St. John's for the tourist to transact all necessary business, after which she sails direct to Pilley's. Our information cost us this cool cash in addition to the three per cent. discount, and we trust those who follow us will profit by the old adage "a penny saved is a penny earned," and avoid our mistake.

After bewailing our misfortune we next started out to hunt up the august personage who was to relieve us each of $100.00 and one hundred cents for a license to permit each to shoot five male and three female caribou, this being the limit allowed by the

GAME LAWS OF NEWFOUNDLAND,

of which we here give a brief summary:

Caribou—Deer Preservation Act of 1889. I. Hereafter no person shall kill any caribou except from the 15th day of September until the 15th day of February, both inclusive. II. No person shall during any one year or season kill more than five stag and three doe caribou. Notwithstanding anything contained in this Act, any poor settler may kill caribou (or deer), for his immediate consumption or that of his family, or may kill for purposes of sale within the Colony during the season, between the 1st of October and the 15th of February, in any year not more than ten caribou (or deer), but not by any snare or trap, or pit, or by the hunting or chasing of dogs.

Non-Resident Licenses — III. No person not actually a resident in this Colony or its dependencies shall kill caribou without having first procured a license for the season, and shall pay for such license an annual sum of $100.00. V. The license required by this Act may be issued by a Stipendiary Magistrate, Collector or Sub-Collector of Customs, a Justice of the Peace, and such other officers or persons as may be empowered by the Governor in Council for that purpose, the person requiring the license paying therefor one dollar.

Exportation — VIII. No person shall export or carry with him out of this Colony any venison or the heads, antlers, skins or other parts of the caribou without first clearing the same at some Custom House.

Dogs — XI. Any person who shall hereafter kill any caribou with dogs shall be liable to a fine of $25.00.

Ptarmigan, Willow Grouse, Partridges — I. No person shall kill any ptarmigan or willow grouse (commonly called partridge) or any other kind of grouse or partridge within this Colony between the 12th of January and the 15th of September.

Migratory Birds—An Act of June 11, 1890, § 2. No person shall kill any curlew, plover, snipe or other wild migratory birds (excepting wild geese) between the 12th day of January and the 20th day of August.

Moose, Elk. V.   No person shall kill any moose or elk for a period of ten years from the 1st of January, 1886.

Rabbit, Hare. VIII.   No person shall kill any wild rabbit or hare from the 1st of March until the 1st of September.

Salmon, Grilse, Par, Trout, Char. 102, § II.   No salmon shall be taken before the 1st day of May or after the 10th day of September.   Trout, char, whitefish, landlocked salmon.   Chapter 7, Laws of 1888, § I. No person shall catch any kind of trout, char, whitefish, landlocked salmon or any fresh water or any migratory fish between the 15th day of September and the 1st day of February.

Soon after starting on our search for the means of complying with this law, we met a policeman, and inquired of him as to who was the proper person to issue our licenses.   He very courteously volunteered to accompany us to the Court House, ushered us in, gave us comfortable seats, and as a cause was being tried we were well entertained as it progressed.   Finally

the Judge postponed the case, when one of the uni-
formed officers of the Court was noticed holding a
short but private whispering conversation with His
Honor, and he at once repaired to an adjoining room
which proved to be his private office, and we were
soon ushered into his august presence.

THE STIPENDIARY MAGISTRATE.

After a greeting only such as a hospitable Newfoundlander and the prospective recipient of $303.00
could accord, he passed the pipe and proceeded to tell
us of the grand sport to be had with rod and gun in
the Colony. In short, he had so much to say and
was wound up so tight, that half an hour had passed
and nothing was done toward filling up our certifi-
cates or licenses. Soon an officer appeared, and after
making a military salute, informed His Honor that
the barristers and their clients were waiting his presence. Somewhat annoyed at being disturbed in his
reverie, he curtly replied, "Let them wait." Seeing
that there was little prospect of getting our licenses
without interfering with the rights of good people in
the court room, the writer suggested that inasmuch as
His Honor's time was valuable and we were obliged
to be loafers until the *Virginia Lake* sailed in five or
six days, we would call at a fixed hour in the after-

noon.   In the mean time he could cause our papers
to be prepared, when it would require but a short
time to arrange our business.   With some hesitancy
he consented, and we bowed ourselves out promising
to call at the appointed hour.   We were on hand at
the time named; he was in his office, and had the
floor covered with six of the finest gray wolf skins we
had ever seen, and upon which he informed us he had
just paid a bounty of $12.00 each.   One of our party
observed that they would make fine robes, when he
remarked with a sly twinkle in his eye that the law
required him to take possession of the pelts in order
that dishonest persons might not collect the bounty a
second time on the same animals!   We were soon re-
lieved of our cash, and in return were each in possession of the following license:

POLICE OFFICE, ST. JOHN'S, NEWFOUNDLAND,

Oct. 6th......1894

According to the provisions of the Act passed in the Fifty-second year of the Reign of Her Majesty, entitled "An Act to provide for the preservation of Deer and the Acts in amendment thereof" permission is hereby given to S. T. Davis M.D. to kill five stag and three are caribou in Newfoundland and its dependencies during the season from the 15th day of September until the fifteenth day of February then next ensuing, both days inclusive, he having paid the license fee of one hundred dollars, and having made oath or affirmation required by the 4th Sec. of the amended Act

O.W. Prowse

Dated at: St. John's this sixth day of October A.D 1894

LICENSE—$100.00 AND 100 CENTS.

In addition to the restrictions contained in the above, we were obliged to subscribe to a written obligation that we would use our utmost endeavors to preserve the flesh of the animals taken. Before leaving, he insisted on us taking tea with him at his villa in the suburbs on the following day (Sunday) between the hours of 3 and 5 P. M.

Sunday, October 7th.   Thermometer 50; clear, pleasant.   This morning we all accompanied our landlady to a Wesleyan church, where a bright Irish minister preached us a good, solid sermon.   The congregation was made up of a good class of people, and from their general appearance there was no mistaking their intelligence and standing in society.   In the afternoon we took a walk to the top of Signal Hill.   This hill is situated on the east side of the channel entrance to the harbor, and is a barren rock with two beautiful little lakes nestling on its western slope just below the crest.

Monday, October 8th.   Thermometer 45; fog in the morning.   As we had not yet laid in our supplies, and from what information we were able to collect concluded that St. John's was the proper place to do so, this day (or as much thereof as was necessary) was set apart for that purpose; and it is but justice to the St. John's merchants to say that no one can go wrong in making purchases of supplies from any of the many retail stores which line Water Street for more than a mile.   We selected Bowring Brothers, where we were well treated and the goods furnished were first-class, fresh and at reasonable prices.

EIGHT MEN FOR TWENTY DAYS.

As our party would consist of the five natives and

three hunters, we had to provide for eight people for the twenty days we intended being away from salt water, on the basis that we would have from the start all the fresh meat we could use; also salt sufficient for table use, as well as the curing of twenty-four hides and heads, in case we should desire to bring that number out. Our past experience proved of value, and enabled us to make ends meet very nicely by purchasing the following articles—the prices being appended to enable those interested to better calculate the expenses of a similar trip:

50 pounds	No. 1 hard bread, @ 7c	....	$3.50
150 "	flour, @ 4c	....	6.00
25 "	corn meal, @ 5c	....	1.25
30 "	roll bacon, @ 25c	....	7.50
30 "	family pork, @ 12c	....	3.60
7 "	coffee, @ 35c	....	2.45
4 "	tea, ½ pound packs, @ 60c	....	2.40
25 "	granulated sugar, @ 10c	....	2.50
5 "	rice, @ 10c	....	.50
5 "	beans, @ 7c	....	.35
½ "	black pepper, @ 20c	....	.10
20 "	onions, @ 5c	....	1.00
4 "	candles, @ 20c	....	.80
10 bags salt, @ 3c		....	.30
3 1-pound cans Royal Baking Powder, @ 20c			.60
1 box matches		....	.15

3 gallons molasses, in 3 stone jugs............... $1.25
1 lantern for candles............................... .75
4 yards oilcloth.................................... 1.25
1 dozen cans milk.................................. 1.80
                                                  _____
                                                   $38.05

Making $12.68 for each man's share, and less than two dollars a day for twenty days for eight men, with appetites like bark mills.

It will be noticed that but few luxuries are included in the forgoing list, and on that account it might not suit the tastes of many. Butter, for example, might have been added, and indeed many other articles, but they would have added considerable weight and very little solid comfort. It will also be noticed that what are known as "wet goods," "snake bite," "tangle foot," etc., are not included in the outfit. We had two half-pint flasks of whiskey with us, to be used for medicinal purposes only, and both were taken back to salt water with the corks undisturbed.

Inasmuch as it was an impossibility to carry our outfit all the way in at one trip, it was evident that what could not be taken had to be cachéd at or near the head of West Pond, the end of water transportation. We therefore had all goods that could be divided put up in four different parcels and packed in four boxes, each box containing as near as possible one of the four parts of each article. These boxes were numbered from one to four and four numbered lists made of their contents.

MISTAKE NO. 3.

Having completed our commissary purchases, we were ready for the next order of business, viz., the procuring for each a pair of sealskin Labrador boots, which we were assured by Wakeman Holbertson, in his description of a hunt in Newfoundland, were the only footwear which could be used. He went even so far as to assert that rubber goods could not be used in Newfoundland. Had he advised *rubber boots* as the only proper footgear to use on a caribou hunt in Newfoundland, he would have saved us from having our six legs pulled to the tune of $2.50 per leg. We got them all right, at $5.00 a pair. True, they are the lightest boot made, and may do on dry ice and in dry snow, but not to wade through water halfway up to the knees. They are as thin as writing paper, and the only way you can put them on is when sopping wet. They are not waterproof according to the American interpretation of the term as we saw it. My friends after testing theirs gave them to the carriers; I brought mine home as a relic, and they are for sale cheap.

SEEING THE CITY.

Tuesday, October 9th — Thermometer, 50; clear. Having attended to all the business matters deemed necessary, this day was set apart for sight-seeing in this land-locked city within sight of the turbulent Atlantic. For picturesqueness of situation there is no

AN OLD VIEW OF ST. JOHN'S.

other city in North America to compare with St. John's. As the voyager coming northward from Cape Race sails along the grim-walled coast, whose rocks tower from two to four hundred feet high and hurl back the waves in defiance, the steamer suddenly turns her prow shoreward, as if to dash herself against the dark cliffs. In a few moments a narrow opening in the rocky wall is seen, as if by some convulsion of nature the great dark rampart had been rent asunder and the sea had rushed in. As the ship glides through this cleft, the traveller looks not without a touch of awe at the great cliffs of dark red sandstone, piled in broken masses on a foundation of gray slate rock. On the right he sees an almost perpendicular precipice 300 feet in height, above which rises with almost equal steepness the crest of Signal Hill, 520 feet above the level of the sea, on which stands the block house for signalling vessels as they approach the harbor. On the left the rugged hill attains a height of six hundred feet; from its base a rocky promontory juts out, forming the entrance to the Narrows on one side. On the summit of this projection is Fort Amherst lighthouse, where is heard the hoarse music of the restless Atlantic, whose waves lash the rocks beneath.

THE NARROWS.

Formerly batteries armed with formidable guns rose one over the other on the projecting shoulders and narrow platforms of the surrounding cliffs, and at the narrowest point a rock above water stands off from the shore known as Chain Rock, where in former times, during the troubles with foreign nations, a huge

FORT AMHERST.

chain stretched across the Narrows, bolted into this rock on one side, and raised or lowered as required by a powerful capstan on the other side, precluded the possible entrance of any hostile fleets.

The Narrows or channel leading to the harbor is nearly half a mile in length, and it is not until two-thirds of it have been passed that the city of 30,000 inhabitants can be seen. At the end of the Narrows the harbor trends suddenly to the west, thus completely shutting out the swell of the ocean. In ten minutes after the bow is turned shoreward the steamer is safely moored in a perfectly land-locked harbor. Vessels of the largest tonnage can enter at all stages of the tide, the rise of which does not exceed four feet.

Between Signal Hill and Fort Amherst, at the entrance, the Narrows are about 1,400 feet in width; and at the narrowest point, between Pancake and Chain Rocks, they are not more than 600 feet wide. The harbor is one mile long, half a mile wide, and 90 feet deep, with mud bottom; and its equal would be hard to find anywhere.

The city is built on the gradually sloping bluff on the north side of the harbor. On top of the slope there is a large level plain, which is occupied by beautiful residences; and still further northward is a stretch of fine agricultural land, divided into many fine farms. The principal streets are Water, Duckworth and Gowen. The new part built since the last great fire in 1892 is considerably improved, and the

ST. JOHN'S BURNT DISTRICT AFTER FIRE OF 1892.

large business houses in the eastern half of Water Street compare favorably with similar structures in cities of the same size in any part of the United States. There is an excellent system of sewerage, and the water supply cannot be excelled. It is obtained from Windsor Lake, four miles distant, the lake being four hundred feet above the level of the sea.

RELATIVE DISTANCES.

St. John's is situated on the east side of the peninsula of Avalon, which presents a wide frontage to the sea and is the portion of North America nearest to the Old World. It is sixty miles north of Cape Race, 600 miles from Halifax, 1,170 miles from Montreal, 1,200 miles from New York and 1,700 miles from Queenstown, being 1,000 miles nearer the latter place than is New York. The codfish and seal industries are well illustrated by a visit to the large warehouses of Baine Johnston, Job, Monroe, Thorburn and many others along the dock.

The post office is a fine commodious structure situated towards the western end of Water Street. The upper floor is devoted to the purposes of a public museum, which we found well worth a visit.

THE MUSEUM.

Here are arrayed specimens of all the minerals and

coals found in the island, as well as building stone, marbles, granites, woods, etc.

The birds, animals and fossil remains of extinct species are well represented, and the antiquarian will find a most interesting collection of relics belonging to the once powerful though now extinct aboriginal inhabitants, the Beothiks, or "Red Indians." Here are skulls and almost complete skeletons of this extinct race, together with their stone implements, arrow heads, gouges, hatchets, etc. The seal industry is well represented here, not only by mounted specimens, but a fine model of a sealing vessel, ice pan and the method of capture in all its phases.

THE DRY DOCK.

Continuing our walk westward, the Long Bridge is reached, near the head of the harbor, where is the dry dock, built of wood and opened in 1884. It is 600 feet long, 83 feet wide and 25 feet deep at low water, and capable of accommodating all but the very largest vessels afloat. It cost $550,000.00.

THE CATHOLIC CATHEDRAL.

This is the largest and most conspicuous building and stands on the summit of the hill overlooking the city. It is in the form of a Latin cross, 237 feet in

THE CATHOLIC CATHEDRAL.

CHURCH OF ENGLAND CATHEDRAL.

length and 180 feet across the transept, with two towers 138 feet high. Adjacent to it are the bishop's palace, St. Bonaventure's college and convent. The whole group of buildings cost over $500,000.00.

CHURCH OF ENGLAND CATHEDRAL.

This building, which stands about halfway up the slope, will be when completed one of the finest ecclesiastical edifices in British America. Unifortunately it was greatly injured by the great fire of 1892, but is being rapidly restored.

THE PARLIAMENT HOUSE.

On the military road along the crest of the ridge stands the Colonial Building, which contains chambers for the two branches of the Legislature, and also most of the public offices. It is 110 feet long and 85 feet wide, and was built in 1847 at a cost of £100,-000. Near it is the

GOVERNMENT HOUSE.

This comfortable residence of the representative of royalty is surrounded by well kept grounds, and though plain in architecture, is a very desirable hab-. itation.

QUIDI VIDI.

Wednesday, October 10th. Thermometer 50; raining by spells, clearing in the afternoon. To-day we

PARLIAMENT HOUSE.

GOVERNMENT HOUSE.

took an interesting walk to another of the points of interest in the suburbs of this quaint city. Those visiting St. John's should not fail to see this interesting little fishing village, Quidi Vidi, only a short walk of half a mile from the city. The road to it leads

QUIDI VIDI.

you past the penitentiary and hospital and along the shore of pretty Quidi Vidi Lake, on which an annual regatta is held and in winter curling tournaments. The village is a counterpart of hundreds which can be seen from the vessel wherever there is a harbor, the entrance to which is large enough to admit of the passage of a fisherman's boat. In this instance the fissure in the rocky wall is not more than from twelve to fifteen feet wide, and the harbor contains scarcely more than an acre of water surface. As seen in the illustration, their little cottages are clinging to the rocky ledges, while the stages where they land their fish project over the water, as well as the "flakes" on which the cod are dried. During the fishing season the whole process of "splitting," "heading" and "salting" can be seen. To add to the picturesqueness of the scene, a little river which flows through Lake Quidi forms a beautiful little cascade as it falls over the rocks into the diminutive harbor.

CHAPTER XIV.

OFF FOR THE HUNT.

Northward 240 Miles More—Arrival at Pilley's Island—Down
Hall's Bay in the *Nipkin*—Mistake No. 4—Hotel Le Buffe
—The Guide and His Family—Forward to West Pond—
Big Marsh—"Grub" or Tea and Tobacco—Our Cabin.

THURSDAY, *October 11th* —Thermometer,
48; clear and pleasant. An early visit to
the Coastal Steamship Company's office had
elicited the welcome information that the *S. S. Virginia Lake* would sail at 11 A. M. We soon had our
dunnage on board, tickets purchased and state rooms
assigned us; and long ere the time for departure we
were on hand, anxious to get off—though the time
spent in St. John's had not hung heavily on our
hands. The *Virginia Lake* is a handsome boat, and
her commander, Capt. Taylor, we found to be one of
the most jovial and accommodating gentlemen we
had met. Nothing was too much trouble for him
when the comfort of his passengers entered into the
question. The illustration shows Mr. Moore, an old
native sea captain, retired, and Captain Taylor of the
Virginia Lake.

10   (137)

TWO OLD NATIVE SALTS.

Friday, October 12th. Thermometer, 40; raining. To-day we passed several icebergs—in fact they could be seen almost at any time during the day.

Saturday, October 13th. Thermometer 40; clear. Arrived at Pool Island at 6 A. M. This is a small town in a fine harbor, and is noted for its being the residence of several wealthy seal captains. The houses are built mostly upon the rocks. One of them, more pretentious than the rest, had transported earth and formed quite a pretty lawn around his residence. This was a charming day, clear and pleasant, enabling us to spend most of the time on deck. During the afternoon we met a string of fishing schooners numbering seventy-five or eighty on their way from the northern fishing grounds; and as the icebergs were still floating by, relieving the monotony, the time passed rapidly and pleasantly.

Sunday, October 14th. Thermometer 56; clear. Steamer called at Franklin Harbor at 8 A. M. As this was our last day aboard, the steward had prepared a special breakfast, the principal dish being fresh codfish heads with cream sauce dressing. It is hardly necessary to say that with our sharpened appetites we were fully competent to do justice to this, one of the luxuries of a Newfoundland epicure. After a delightful sail of two hours after breakfast, the ship's course became more and more tortuous as she glided through narrow channels between islands, and the repeated orders "A little more to starboard, Sir," and "A little more to larboard, Sir," of the old salt at the wheel more frequent. We were delighted at the sudden appearance of open water hemmed in by a rock-bound coast, and at 11:30 A. M. we were at the docks

AT PILLEY'S ISLAND.

We had been in communication with Mr. H. M. Herbert, who has charge of the Pilley's Island Pyrites

Co. store, and who was on the dock at the time of our arrival.   We were not long in making arrangements with him and the manager of the mine to send us down to the head of Hall's Bay (25 miles), in their beautiful little steam launch "*Nipkin*" for a consideration of $10.00.

DOWN HALL'S BAY IN THE NIPKIN.

By the time we had made arrangements for the launch, the guide, Richard Le Buffe, showed up as per previous arrangement to meet us at Pilley's Island, and this proved to be

MISTAKE NO. 4,

inasmuch as he was three days from home, for which time we paid $3.00 a day.   It was not long before we had ourselves and baggage on board, and at 2:45 P. M. our Captain (Mr. Colburn, the mine boss) sounded the whistle, opened the valve and in the presence of about half the population of the island we steamed off down the bay at the rate of six miles an hour, arriving at the head of the bay at 7:35 P. M.   The whistle was sounded when within about a mile of our landing place, which brought two boats manned by our carriers, who soon transferred ourselves and baggage to shore and within fifty yards of our guide's cabin.

The voyage down the bay was very attractive, the coast scenery being so different in the northern peninsula from that of the southern. In the southern half of the island the coast is little but barren rocks, while

HOTEL LE BUFFE, HALL'S BAY.

north of Bonavista Bay the hills are covered with a profuse growth of foliage, and in the fall months the autumn leaves, interspersed with the deep dark green of the fir, juniper and cedars, present beautiful pictures not soon to be forgotten. The afternoon was one of the choicest, the air pure and invigorating, and both shores of the bay (owing to its narrowness) being within sight, we all enjoyed to the fullest extent the ride down. To add to the picturesqueness of the scenery, every now and then the sleek heads, with human-like eyes, of the bay seal would bob up, take in the situation and duck, reappearing fifty to a hundred and fifty yards away.

AT HOTEL LE BUFFE.

Richard Le Buffe is by birth a French Canadian, and has been a resident of Newfoundland for over twenty years; about forty-two years of age, strong, wiry and rather intelligent and untiring in his efforts to anticipate the wants of his employers; and if the bivouac is crowded he will curl himself up like a dog and sleep beside the fire rather than crowd the mourners. As a still hunter he cannot be excelled; he understands every trick pertaining to his craft, and invariably divines the intentions of the leader of a herd of the great deer from their maneuvering, though a mile off. His family consists of a wife and four children, three little girls and a small boy. The wife is a daughter of "old man Goodyear," who lives in a little cove several miles up the bay—a native Newfoundlander, whose whole life has been spent in seal and cod fishing; and although nearly seventy years of age he served as cook and carrier for our outfit, and stood up under as heavy a load as any of the rest. Mrs. Le Buffe is a good Christian woman and a member of the Church of England; and although she has not had an opportunity of attending church for seven years, her children are required to go to prayers twice a day and those of them who are old enough are familiar with the creed. The shriek of the *Nipkin's* whistle was also a signal for this good housewife, and by the time we had our dunnage unloaded and taken care of, she had hot biscuit, molasses, tea and other viands in readiness, and the hungry crowd soon felt the better of a square meal. After tea, a general pow-wow and smoke followed, and by 10:30 we retired to a temporary bed, made on the floor of the cabin.

Monday, October 15th. Thermometer 60 at 6 P. M. All were up at 5 A. M., and to our great disappointment found a good rain on. Decided not to move until the weather cleared up, which it did at 2 P. M., and we had some sport duck and snipe shooting on the bay head. In the meantime the carriers moved our goods and chattels up West Pond Brook, three miles to the foot of West Pond, where they were cachéd under the canoes and oilcloth mentioned under the head of supplies. It will be noticed that under that head potatoes, or "spuds," as they are called in

Newfoundland, were not mentioned. These were furnished by Le Buffe, from a fine crop of good varieties and fine specimens.

Tuesday, October 16th. Thermometer 48; clear. All hands were up at 4 A. M., and by five we were on the march, and reached the foot of the pond in the gray of the morning. Soon our outfit was loaded, and the five miles up the pond was made at a good pace. There being no wind the water was as placid as a mill

Martin Williams. Jas. Sanders.   Rich. LeBuff.   Indian Jim. Rich. Goodyear.

OUR NATIVE CARRIERS AND GUIDE.

pond. Arriving at the head of the pond we proceeded up the Brook about a mile, or as far as it is navigable for canoes during low water. Here we cachéd our supplies, each hunter carrying in his pack about twenty-five pounds besides his gun, the guide and carriers taking the stove and one package of supplies, besides our personal baggage, bedding, etc. Neither the guide nor carriers took guns, as the hunters are supposed to do all the shooting. The trail was good, with but two or three short hills until we arrived at the foot of the Big Marsh, some three miles from camp. This was laborious tramping, as without a load an ordinary sized man would sink to the ankles in the ooze at every step. During the whole day we made short marches of a mile and a half or two miles, when a halt would be made; and half a dozen times during the journey the natives would "bile the kittle," as they call making tea. Give a Newfoundlander his choice between plenty of grub and no tea and tobacco, or tea and tobacco and no grub, and it would take him but a moment to decide in favor of the tea and tobacco. We arrived at

OUR CABIN ON THE BIG MARSH

just before sundown, giving us ample time to prepare supper, add fresh boughs to the sleeping apartment,

CABIN ON THE BIG MARSH.   (See map for location.)

etc., and as we were all tired, we slept the sleep of the just.

And now, being fairly on the ground, we will devote the concluding chapter to the record of the hunt proper, hoping that our success and our enjoyment of it may lead many others to follow our example.

CHAPTER XV.

HE pages of this concluding chapter have
been purposely held closely to the notes
made at the time on the spot. Imagina-
tion has no place here; the trophies are pictured by
unflattering sunlight, the originals are in our possession, to be freely exhibited to the inquiring guest.
We give the record as it is, believing the class we hope

to have as readers will thus receive most pleasure and benefit.

Wednesday, October 17th. Thermometer 40; threatening. The cook had no difficulty in awakening any of the party for breakfast by daylight; all were astir. Kepler, "the Kid" (J. W. Davis) and LeBuffe started out for fresh meat, while the writer took charge of the carriers and put the camp in shape. The cabin was a compromise between a lean-to and a regular log cabin. The roof was leaky, and the smoke-hole had to be closed. The rear wall, which was only about eighteen inches from the ground, was built up to four feet; a new birch-bark roof was put on, a stone platform was built for the stove, and it was put up; "splits" were secured, and from them tables were made, which were covered with birch bark. The tent was pitched, and surplus goods were stored therein. As the camp was located in the edge of the timber fronting the marsh, a fairly good view of the latter could be had from the immediate vicinity of the cabin; and during the day the writer and the other men at work saw nineteen caribou passing on the opposite side of the marsh, some three-quarters of a mile distant.

Rain began to fall about noon, and the party who went out after meat came into camp empty-handed, though reporting having seen eighteen caribou, but out of range.

Thursday October 18th.—Thermometer 52 ; threatning. Kep and the Kid, guided by Le Buffe, went down the marsh about three-quarters of a mile to what is known as the "lower lookout." These "lookouts" are certain trees which the guides have trimmed up in a convenient manner for climbing, and at some vantage point where a good view can be had of the marsh. The lower lookout consists of a scraggy pine about fifteen inches in diameter and some thirty feet high, standing in a point of timber in a somewhat elevated position. The guide would climb the tree, sit in a crotch formed by the trunk and a branch, and with a field glass he was enabled to scan the marsh from one side to the other, as well as a mile above and below. When he sighted the game, he invariably called out "Deer on the mash?" and when he had satisfied himself as to what lead they were likely to take, he slid down the tree like a cat, and keeping one of the many small islands scattered over the marsh between him and his quarry, he would bid the hunters follow and imitate his movements, which would consist of running, sneaking, walking and crawling in his endeavors to intercept the game, in which he usually succeeded.

The writer selected a point some five hundred yards in front of the cabin and about the middle of the marsh, near a well used trail, and which afterwards became known as "The Doctor's Blind," and is well

"THE DOCTOR'S BLIND."

shown in the illustration. A tree had been blown down, leaving nothing but an upturned decayed root. By placing boughs in front and sticking others upright in the root, a first-class blind was made; and to make it perfect a temporary seat was added.

To return to the day's hunt the writer saw sixteen, killed a fine fat barren doe and wounded a young stag; Kep killed a fine doe and the Kid killed a fair stag, with a good set of antlers, at a single shot— which was, by the way, the first member of the deer family he had ever shot at. They reported having seen twelve in all.

All hands were in camp by 3 P. M., and it is needless to say that thereafter fresh meat was plenty in camp, and the natives were "scaffling," some for their winter's meat, 'which they took out with their dog sledges after the snow came and the streams and lakes were frozen over.

It might be well to state here that the middle of October is about the height of the rutting season, and the old stags are not fit for food, their flesh being so musky that it is impossible to use it.

Friday, October 19th. Thermometer 35; threatening. LeBuffe and the writer hunted west to what is known as Hamah's Lookout, two and a-half miles. We sighted but eight deer, and on our return to camp I shot a fine doe. Kep and Jimmy Goodyear (or, as he will be known hereafter, "Indian Jim") went still farther west, two and a-half miles, to what is called "Grandfather's Lookout."

The Kid remained in camp and paid some attention to the home marsh, but no deer passed. By the middle of the afternoon we were all in, and as the deer were not travelling it was an uneventful day.

As reference has been made to Indian Jim acting as guide to Mr. Kepler, it is well to state that he is a character, and deserves more than passing notice. He is twenty-three years old, stands six feet in his moccasins, straight as an arrow, and lithe as a catamount. He was born in the little cove where his father still resides, and is a child of nature, knowing little or nothing of the ways of civilization. Most of his life has been spent with the neighboring Micmac Indians, and from the time he could follow has accompanied them on their annual fall hunts for meat and hides; and when older he spent his summers either alone or in company with one or two Indians, travelling through the interior with gun, traps and provisions— the latter consisting mostly of tea and tobacco—in search of fur-bearing animals for their pelts. In his excursions he would often be absent from home six weeks or two months. If in a good locality and the tea or tobacco ran short, Jimmy would think nothing of travelling without a compass through the unbroken wilderness forty or fifty miles in search of the needful commodities. He can call the sly beaver to within a rod of his regulation muzzle-loading smoothe-bore gun, handle a canoe like an Esquimaux his kayak, and still hunt like a panther. In wood-craft he has nothing to learn, having practiced all its tricks from childhood, including the incantations and superstitious ceremonies of his dark-skinned tutors; and withal he is as gentle as a lamb, truthful and obedient.

Saturday, October 20. Thermometer 32; windy and clear. Ice one-eighth inch thick, which is the first

INDIAN JIM.

we have seen except in the shape of bergs on our way up the coast. The writer occupied the blind on the home marsh a short time in the forenoon, and an hour and a-half in the afternoon; saw six deer, but as they were not ornamented with antlers they were allowed to pass, though within easy range. "The Kid" and Le Buffe went south a short distance, saw fourteen, had one shot but missed—a fine head. Indian Jim and Kep went west, saw three deer in short range, heads no good; reserved fire.

At first we were shooting for meat; now as we must not shoot more than the eight allowed by law, it dawns upon us that none but representative heads must be shot at, or somebody will get left when the trophies come to be counted. Twenty-three seen in all to-day.

Sunday, October 21st. Thermometer 32; cloudy and high wind. Moderated toward evening and began raining. All remained in camp to-day. But four deer passed the camp, two of them within range.

Monday, October 22d.—Thermometer 37; misty. Kep and Le Buffe went down the marsh, saw eight deer and could have killed two. The Kid and Jimmy saw twenty-three, but did not shoot, though they filed past them within thirty yards. The writer saw three and could have killed two but did not.

Tuesday, October 23d.—Thermometer 32; clear. The writer watched his blind in the morning, and saw but one deer which was in range but allowed to pass. In the afternoon went to South Hills near camp, and could have killed two does. Indian Jim and the Kid went south this morning and returned before noon, the Kid walking proudly and Indian Jim bending under the weight of two immense antlered heads. As this was the Kid's red letter day the author will allow him to tell how it happened :

" Jim was a few steps ahead, no deer were in sight from the Lower Lookout, and as the main lead to the South Hills opened into the Big Marsh just below the Lower Lookout tree, he swung his long right arm to the right, pointing down a little stream, as he said : 'We walk half an hour, find big grandfather stag.' 'All right, Jim, we will walk.' Half an hour later found us passing out of a little valley into a large marsh, or rather series of marshes. Just then three deer, all does, rounded a little point of woods. Jim crouched down on the marsh, and the deer came toward us at a slow walk until within seventy-five yards, when they began to be suspicious and halted. As we had plenty of meat and the deer had no antlers, I did not intend killing any, but was just admiring their sleek, round bodies when Jim's Indian instincts got the better of him and he whispered to me, 'Umph! you only kill one deer. I like to have her to eat this winter; nice, fat'—at the same time pointing to a fine doe in the lead. 'Well, Jim, I'll try'—raising my gun as I spoke. The deer saw the movement and turned to flee, but it was too late; the leaden messenger had found the fatal spot in the fore shoulder, and the doe rolled over. A few bounds and Jim was astride of her, and his long knife was letting her lifeblood out. In a few moments the doe was disemboweled and placed out of the reach of 'varmints,' where it would remain until the snow came, when Jim with his dogs and sled would transport it to his humble cabin nearly thirty miles distant. Soon we were on our way. 'Never mind,' says Jim; 'find big grandfather stag by-un-by.' We had not travelled more than fifty yards until Jim dropped to the ground, I doing the same; and trying to imitate the movements of a serpent we crawled into some bushes near by. Jim craned his long neck out, while I lay close to the ground and he counted 'one, two, three, four, five—fifteen—old grandfather stag behind. Wait.' Turning my head I could see the feet of the passing herd about fifty yards away. Suddenly Jim parted the bushes and said, 'there un big stag, sir.' Taking a quick but careful aim, I dropped him with a shot behind the shoulders. Twice he tried to rise, when Jim said, 'Shoot' gin, sir' which I did, and the second ball sent him to the happy hunting grounds. This stag, which would have weighed at least 650 pounds, was the largest I killed, and had a magnificent head of horns. Jim soon had him turned bottom side up ready to dress, when looking up the marsh, half a mile distant I saw an immense stag with antlers like a brush heap. 'Jim! Jim!' I exclaimed—and away he ran, and I after him, through the woods, over a little marsh into another little woods, where we crawled up to a herd twenty-two in number. The deer were feeding, but soon became aware that something was near that boded no good and began to edge off, and as they advanced, kept looking back. I could have killed a doe several times, but I was after horns; but to save me I could not get a shot at the old stag. At last they reached the open marsh and stood like frightened cattle. The old warrior turned broadside, and stepping on a rock near by, I raised on tip-toe, fired over the back of a doe, and had the satisfaction of seeing my stag drop dead. He had the largest antlers I secured. As we ran out on the marsh to claim our prize, the remainder of the herd ran off about a hundred yards and halted. A fine barren doe almost as white as snow took Jim's

THE KID'S TROPHIES OF THE HUNT.

eye, and he repeated his old story about winter's meat and buckskin for moccasins as he glanced from the doe to me. 'Him a fat un,' said he. Only three inches of the deer's shoulder was visible as she stood by the side of a tree. 'Jim, I might miss.' 'No; un gun shoot where un held. You an me find more big stag by-un-by.' Resting on one knee, I held just near the bark of the tree, and at the report of the gun the doe fell dead. I sat down on a rock watching Jim dress the deer, when all at once I heard a great racket in my rear. I sprang to my feet to find a herd of deer not twenty yards off on a full run; in another instant they would have been over us. On seeing us they turned off, and there being no horns among them, they were allowed to go unmolested. I then looked at my watch and saw that in forty-five minutes I had killed four deer and seen fifty-one."

Kep and Le Buffe started for the Lower Lookout, and here the author will allow Kep to tell how he killed the wrong deer and missed adding a fine pair of antlers to his list of trophies:

"About 11 A. M. we spied fifteen deer in one drove about half a mile distant, feeding and moving slowly around the point of a thickly wooded island. Le Buffe, who was perched high up on the tree, watched them very intently through the glass for quite a while,

trying to make out the direction they were aiming for
as they circled over the marsh. 'There's one awful
big one, with dandy horns,' said Le Buffe, as he came
down the tree like a streak of greased lightning and
beckoned me to follow him as he ran down in the direction of the caribou, keeping well under cover and
as near the edge of the marsh as possible till we got
about halfway to them. We then had to cut across
a small island in order to keep under cover and to
windward of them. I was panting for breath by the
time we got through the terrible thicket; and there
in full sight, only about a hundred yards distant,
stood the whole flock in a bunch. 'Keep close to
the ground and try to get a shot at that big fellow
in the middle if you can,' whispered Le Buffe. I
wanted him badly, but he kept well in the centre of
the herd, as they moved uneasily around as if they
scented danger, and grouped in such a way that it
was hard to get a shot at him. Several times I was
on the point of pulling the trigger as he presented his
head and neck above the others. 'What do you
think?' said I to Le Buffe. 'Well, I would wait a bit:
don't shoot till you get a good chance at his shoulders.'
I was watching intently for that chance as the herd
kept moving about and gradually getting a little further away from us, and I was getting extremely anx-

ious, fearing that the monarch of the party might get away after all. Finally I caught a glimpse of his monstrous head as he moved a little to one side, and the next instant I glanced through the sights and fired at what I supposed was his big white shoulder. At the crack of the rifle Le Buffe jumped to his feet and shouted, ' You missed him—there he goes—try him again on the run!' I saw my mistake, and fired at him as he was pulling out with the rest of the herd, as they helterskeltered over the wet marsh at a tremendous gait, making the water fly as high as a two-story house in their mad flight; but I only succeeded in wounding him slightly. We then took an inventory of what I had done with my first shot, and found that I had hit two caribou —one a large stag, but with comparatively small horns, and killed the other a doe. 'I am sorry the big one got away,' said the guide. I was so mortified at my loss and mistake that I don't think I spoke six words on our way back to the lookout. It was then about the middle of the day and Le Buffe 'biled the kittle.' After lunch he climbed the tree again, and a short time afterward we both noticed a little smoke curling through the trees at the head of a small island in the marsh, about three-quarters of a mile distant. Le Buffe discovered, with the aid of the glass, that it

WM. PAUL.

was our old friend Wm. Paul, the Micmac Indian, with two squaws and two half-grown boys, who were on the trail leading to their camp near by, and had stopped to take a rest and 'bile the kittle.' While Le Buffe was watching the Indians' actions I noticed two fine caribou on the marsh, moving directly towards old Paul and his party. 'Now,' said Le Buffe, 'look sharp and we may see some fun.' Nearer and nearer went the two deer toward the curling smoke, seeming not to notice till within fifty paces of it, when they both stopped with heads erect, and stood as if paralyzed at what they saw.   The next instant I saw a little puff of smoke from old Paul's six-foot muzzle-loading gun, and a convulsive leap into the air by one of the deer followed by a loud report like blasting rocks.   'There, he has wounded

WM. PAUL'S SISTER.

one of them and scared the other almost to death,'
said Le Buffe. 'Yes,' he continued, 'it is trying hard to get to its feet again, but can't.' In the
meantime Paul loaded his old gun and fired another
slug into the wounded animal; then the whole party
broke cover, and with an Indian yell of triumph ran
out to the fallen deer, which was still trying hard to
rise as the Indians surrounded it. 'Thud! Thud!
Poonk! Poonk!' came a peculiar sound over the
marsh, while they kept up their infernal yelling.
'What are they doing now?' I asked Le Buffe (who
could see every move they made, owing to his elevated position and having the field glass.) 'Oh, the
dirty old heathen is mauling it to death with the butt
of his old musket,' he replied, as he slid down the
tree; 'come let us go down and see what they are
doing.' By the time we got there they had the hide
almost off, and so intent were they on their work that
they scarcely noticed our presence, as each one pulled
and tugged at it wherever they could get a hold, chattering all the while like a flock of crows. We remained to see them dress the deer and cook the
dainty bits of offal, consisting of the 'bombgut' or
rectum and the marrow bones—the latter having
been roasting over the hot coals since they were cut
off, and the boys were soon quarreling as they cracked

them between stones, each fearing that one might get
a morsel more than the other. Old Paul and the
squaws were gorging themselves from the contents
of the kettle, which contained scraps of offal scarcely
warmed through. We declined a very cordial invitation to take a snack with them, on general principles, and compromised the matter by furnishing
them with sufficient 'backy' to fill their pipes all
round. On the way up the marsh I had an opportunity of killing a fine two-year-old stag, but as my
ideas of antlers had enlarged very materially, and his
were small, I allowed him to go on his way undisturbed. We proceeded to the lookout, where we had
been but a few minutes when the "Kid" and Indian
Jim came round the point from the South Hills. The
latter had on his broad shoulders two beautiful heads.
'Aha! I see you have had good luck,' said I. 'Oh,
yes,' replied the Kid, with a beaming countenance, 'I
never had so much fun in all my life! We saw fifty-
one caribou, and I killed four of them—two big stags
and two fat does. 'We are the champions now, and
and don't you forget it, 'said Indian Jim with a satisfied look as he filled his pipe. After congratulations
all around, we pulled out for the cabin."

We had a big day, as the party saw eighty-four deer
in all; and as the Kid was the hero, we were obliged

to give him plenty of elbow room at the supper table, to make up the bunk without his assistance, and to yield him several inches more space in it for the night. And as Indian Jim's spirits were at high tide, he entertained us far into the night with accounts of his life and adventures with the Micmacs—how they lived, cooked, slept, hunted, trapped, danced, married, fought, worshipped, buried the dead, etc., and how he himself had hunted the great deer, beaver, seals, otter, owls, grouse, foxes, bears and wolves—the flesh of all of which he declared to be good to eat "if a man was hungry."

Wednesday, October 24th. Thermometer 30; clear. As Indian Jim desired to complete the "scaffling" of the two fat does killed by the Kid yesterday, the writer went with him. Saw seven and could have killed three, but as they were does and stags with comparatively small antlers, the opportunities were allowed to pass with the deer. Returned to camp by late dinner time; and as Martin Williams had completed skinning out the Kid's two stag heads, and the curing of the skins fell to the writer's lot, they were attended to during the afternoon.

Here it might be well to state that the skinning out of the head of one of these great deer is quite a task, and great care and judgment must be exercised, or when the specimen comes to be mounted it will be impossible for the taxidermist to do justice to the subject. Martin Williams, with a little instruction as to the nose and ears, became very expert, and would be worth more than his wages for that purpose alone. Even after the head skin is off it is no small job to clean the skull properly. The brain must be thoroughly removed, as well as every particle of flesh, and the cavity of the nostrils must be well swabbed out. After all this has been attended to the salt, alum and arsenic mixture used in curing the skins should be applied and the specimen placed in as dry a place as the accommodations afford, with a free circulation of air. In the curing of the head skins the writer uses the following mixture, which gives the very best results in any cimate:

Fine salt...................................6 ounces.
Pulverized alum ....2 ounces.
Arsenic...................................1 ounce.
    Mix well.

As soon as the skin has been removed from the animal, or before it has become dry, rub the powder into the flesh side well, being very careful to see that it has been well applied to the very edges of the skin, as well as the lips, eyelids and the everted ears. After every portion has been gone over and well rubbed in, fold the skin together in such a manner that the flesh sides shall come in contact, then roll tightly together and secure the bundle with twine. The skin is then ready to be packed away, one roll against another, and better on the ground, covering the whole well with green boughs. In forty-eight hours open them up, hang them in the shade, but where they get a free circulation of air, and in fair dry weather the skins will be dry and can safely be packed in bales, and when the taxidermist or tanner relaxes them the hair will be found tight and the pelt in first-class condition. Out of the twenty-one head skins brought out by our party, there was not a square inch of hair slipped.

Kep, the Kid and Le Buffe spent part of the day at the Lower Lookout, sighting seven deer, but as they were not the kind they were looking for, they were not disturbed.

Thursday, October 25th. Thermometer 35; clear and windy. The writer having sprained his ankle yesterday, did not get farther than the blind across the marsh. Saw four deer killing a fine stag with fair antlers under the following circumstances: The deer were feeding along slowly with the wind, just right, one path of the trail passing within twenty feet of the blind. The deer were slow in coming up, which gave ample opportunity to examine the stag's antlers with the glass, and the same time to arrive at the conclusion that he was not wanted. As he approached still nearer, and when within about fifty yards of the blind, it was noticed that he took the trail which passed within twenty feet of it. The temptation was too great, and he lost his life by exciting a desire in the heart of the hunter to kill a wild caribou at twenty feet, and find out whether at such short range the ball would pass through the animal. When directly opposite the blind the trigger was pressed. The ball, 40–65 Winchester, passed in between two ribs just back of the point of the foreshoulder on the left side, passing through and striking the centre of the rib on the opposite side, which it failed to break. See Illustration, Fig. 3. Fig.

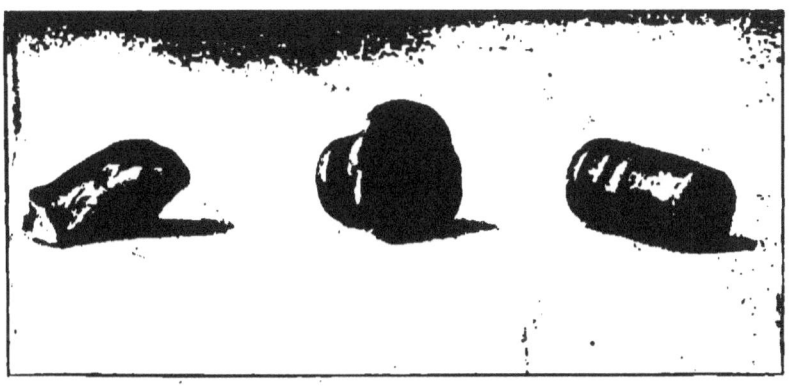

Fig. 1.   Fig. 2.   Fig. 3.

BULLETS.

1 passed through both shoulder blades of a large stag at a distance of three hundred paces, and was found lodged against the skin. Fig. 2 passed through between two ribs, struck an opposite rib breaking it at a distance of 150 paces.

Kep and Le Buffe were north of the camp part of the day and killed a barren doe with fine head. The Kid and Jimmy were south, and killed a stag and barren doe.

Friday, October 26th. Thermometer 45; cloudy in the morning, but cleared up soon, and became a beautiful bright day. We had now been in the hunt ten days, and had secured some fine heads, but not all we desired. By this time Kep was getting in fine shape for hunting, and seemed more like the same "Black Fox" of years ago when we made many a tramp together, when game was plenty in the western counties of Pennsylvania.

The programme for the day's hunt was outlined the day before. Kep and Le Buffe were to get an early start and make a reconnoitering tour to "Grandfather's Lookout," and if possible push farther into the White Hills, as we were all extremely anxious to secure fine large stag heads, as well as three antlered cows. The Kid and writer were to remain at the main camp and keep watch over the passers-by. Our end of the line did not pan out well, as not a deer was sighted; but Kep and Le Buffe had

A RED LETTER DAY.

And here is the way Kep tells it: " We took a different route to reach the hills, and saw on our way up quite a number of caribou, as we circled round through the 'Big Marsh,' thick wooded islands and small lakes, and could have killed a number of them; but nothing suited us. About noon we stopped to 'bile the kittle,' and enjoy our tea, sea-biscuit and cold venison as only hungry hunters in a bracing atmosphere and after a long tramp can. As we were enjoying our snack, Le Buffe ever on the alert, saw a very large stag alone about three-quarters of a mile distant, feeding by the side of a small lake. As we observed him through the glass, we discovered that he had a fine head, just such as we were looking for; but the great trouble was to get within gun-shot, as there was little available cover, and the wind was against us. We succeeded, however, in getting within 250 yards of him without much trouble, and then crawled through the wet marsh grass about seventy-five yards further. Here even the grass was absent, and I was obliged to try a long shot. After recovering my wind a little after the sneak and crawl, I took very careful aim, and as the rifle cracked the great animal made a lunge forward and fell dead. Of course I felt elated, and Le Buffe put his big hand in mine, congratulating me on the fine shot and the beautiful trophy.

"After skinning him, Le Buffe shouldered the head and hide, and we proceeded on our way toward the height of land or what is known as the Barrens. When we reached 'Hanah's Lookout' we rested, and left the head until our return. We were about two and a-half miles west of our cabin, but there was still a higher point about two miles distant in the direction of the famous 'Topsails,' which if we could reach it would afford us a magnificent view of the country, and put us in the very heart of the best hunting grounds. We pushed on and arrived at our destination, "Grandfather's Lookout," about 3 P. M. It was a beautiful sight as we stood on this high ledge of rocks overlooking the high tableland in the heart of the rolling moss covered 'White Hills.' A short distance westward were the three Topsail peaks, looming up like great castles or icebergs in the clear atmosphere. North and south, the unique gray hills as far as the eye could see, and to the eastward, we could look down on the many wooded islands and small lakes dotted over the great marshes, Barney's Brook,

West Pond, and the 'tickles' leading into the bay at Pilley's Island.

"But near us to the eastward, within a mile, was to me a much more interesting picture. On the plain below us were more than a hundred caribou, moving about among the little moss-covered knolls, rocks and tufts of scraggy evergreens of fir and juniper. As I brought my field-glass to bear upon the scene, I beheld a picture which I shall never forget. About half a mile down the slope, in a small open marsh, were at least fifty caribou gathered in a crowd, and right in the centre was a battle royal between several great stags for supremacy and possession of the favored does. The battle seemed to be waged principally against one great kingly-looking fellow with magnificent antlers. The does with their fawns and the yearlings (prickets) and younger stags had apparently formed a ring or circle around the half-dozen or more fierce combatants in their great struggle for the survival of the fittest—the does venturing in near them now and then seemingly to encourage the fighters by their presence. The clashing of their horns could be easily heard as they plunged and reared at each other in deadly strife. The weaker gradually succumbed one by one and were eventually driven off, leaving the 'king' master of the situation. But his glory was destined to be short lived; little did he know that there was danger near, and that his kingly head should soon fall, as a specimen and trophy of the noblest of his kind.   It was now quite late in the afternoon, and as we were about five miles from camp as the raven flies, and several more by the roundabout way we were obliged to take to reach our cabin, Le Buffe thought it was too late to begin shooting; the weather was mild, and the deer would not travel; better go to camp and return in the morning with the whole outfit, put up a temporary camp, and remain until we had filled out our string of heads allowed by law.   But what sportsman could turn his back on such a picture without making an attempt to secure the head of the king? I suggested that we should try for it, even at the risk of camping out.   This was easier said than done, as there were several small groups of deer between us and the herd in which he was presiding, and many sharp eyes and noses to be feared.   Le Buffe was fearful that if they should detect us either by sight or scent we might stampede the whole party and lose all, though he was willing to make the effort.

"We started out very cautiously, creeping through the low cover and keeping as well to windward of them as possible, gradually getting nearer the point of attack.   When within about 400 yards we thought

KEPLER AND THE KING.

all was lost, as a big stag close by, which had been whipped, discovered us and created quite a disturbance by his loud grunts as he kept trotting backwards and forwards from group to group, trying to give the alarm; but as there was another fight on be-

low him, the main herd's attention was attracted to
that, and no stampede occurred just then.   From this
point forward the cover was so light that we had to
worm along very close to the ground part of the way,
through water and muck, regardless of wet knees and
elbows; but finally succeeded in getting within about
225 paces of the 'king;' but here the cover ended and
our position on sloping ground exposed us to the deer,
and I was obliged to try my hand again at long range.
I raised the sights for the estimated distance as well
as I could, and as I was lying down, took very careful
aim from an elbow rest, military style.   I fired,
and as the rifle cracked I saw that the ball had
struck him too far back; it seemed to make him perfectly ferocious, as he crippled around in the herd with
a broken thigh, still holding the fort against all comers.
He soon turned a broadside, and I fired again with
better results; he made a few wicked lunges in the
direction of one of his late rivals, and fell dead.   We
then broke cover and ran down to where the fallen
hero lay; and strange to say, the herd seemed to be
panic-stricken at the downfall of their leader—some
of them trotting around close by, and others standing
as if paralyzed within easy shot.   Just then I noticed
a large stag standing about eighty yards off with a
magnificent head of antlers.   I shot him down in

THE "KING."

his tracks. At this stage of the game all seemed to be in confusion, as the deer did not seem to know what the shooting meant. As Le Buffe did not carry a gun, to keep out of my way and out of sight of the game he had taken shelter behind a large rock about the size of an old fashioned Pennsylvania bake-oven (such as our ancestors used), about 200 yards from where I was doing the shooting. Here he almost came to grief, as he was attacked by a fierce caribou with most vicious horns. His cry for help attracted my attention just in time to save him, as the maddened beast was grunting and charging at him as he was running round and round the rock. I ran down to within about twenty yards of the circus, when the enraged animal caught sight of me and immediately squared off to give me battle on open ground, and looked as if he asked no favor under the circumstances. But I had him well covered with the rifle, and called out to Le Buffe to lie flat behind the rock as I was going to shoot. Just as the great savage deer lowered his head to make a rush at me, I fired a ball into his breast, and he fell dead within six feet of Le Buffe—who is a brave man and used to danger, but at this moment was as white as a sheet as he again took me by the hand.

"This over, and before we had time to consider what

next, we noticed a flock of about a dozen deer a short distance off, coming directly towards us. Half of them were stags, with good horns and beautiful white necks. We lay down behind the dead fighter, and in a few seconds the leader was within thirty feet of us; and as they paraded by I picked out the one with the finest horns and let him down. The rest ran off a short distance, circled around, and stopped within easy gunshot. This last shot completed my eight stags and three female caribou, allowed by law; and the only regret I had was that the Doctor and the Kid were not with us. It was now 4 P. M. and we hurriedly disemboweled the deer and struck for camp, anxious to cover as much of the distance as possible before darkness covered that part of the earth's surface. Unfortunately we had the worst part of the trail to go over last, and night caught us too soon. Several times we lost our course; and as the trail was over the marsh, which is very treacherous, we had a sorry time of it. It was impossible to tell the difference between a puddle of water and a stone, but at last we did reach camp, wet, hungry and foot-sore, but not tired—on! no, not after such a day's sport—but in fine shape to get outside of a big supper which Pap Goodyear had waiting for us. After supper we recounted the incidents of the day. I wrote up my notes, we planned the next day's hunt, and retired to pleasant dreams."

It is hardly necessary to say that Kep, like the Kid after his red-letter day, required extra cover, bunk-room and waiting on. Over a hundred deer seen to-day.

Saturday, October 27th. Thermometer 40; some fog on marsh. As prearranged last night, Le Buffe, Indian Jim, Kep, the Kid and the writer made an early start for the scene of yesterday's hunt, prepared with tent, provisions and cooking utensils, to remain over night or longer if need be. The Kid was entitled to one stag more, and the writer to four. By 10:30 A. M. we were at "Grandfather's Lookout," selected a camping place, and while Indian Jim put up the tent we "biled the kittle," roasted some venison on the ends of sticks and got ourselves in shape for the missing specimens. Before we were through, however, with our impromptu meal, Le Buffe with two smoking ribs in his fist had gone a few yards above us where a better view could be had, and soon sung out, "Deer on the ma'sh," when we all advanced to where he was, and sure enough there on a hillside, all of a mile distant, was a herd of some thirty-five or forty, stringing along unconscious of danger. We were on the top of the height of land on one side of a depression or scoop-out, while they were on the opposite side; and as there was scarcely any cover on either, it required considerable engineering to get even within long range. From where we were it was impossible to determine how many stags were among them, or the size and character of their antlers. There was only one point near the edge of the marsh where two or three small evergreens were standing, which if one could reach it might afford a chance for a shot if the deer kept moving on parallel with the opposite crest of the ridge, provided we were not scented or seen.

After looking the situation over carefully, Le Buffe and the writer began the approach by taking advantage of everything in the shape of cover which it was possible to use; and after a tedious and circuitous route we at last reached the evergreen trees. As the deer were feeding along very slowly, and were unconscious of our presence, we had ample time to examine them carefully through the glass before they came to a point opposite us. We were not long in selecting from among some half dozen stags the one which appeared to have the best pair of antlers, and was the nearest to us. There was a large bowlder which looked as if it had been at some time dropped by an iceberg about opposite where we were, and we calculated the distance to be between 275 and 300

yards. The stag was or seemed to be walking directly
for the rock, and feeling confident that he would
walk up to within a few feet of it and stop, we decided to try him at that point. True to his instinct,
and our surmises based upon previous observation, he
did stop, and gazed curiously and intently at the
rock. I brought the crosshairs to bear on a point
just back of his fore shoulder, pressed the trigger, and
had the satisfaction of seeing him squat. Le Buffe
said, "You hit him all right, but low." The deer
turned to the right and walked about twenty-five
yards away from us, lay down, but immediately got
up and stood broadside. "Give him another, or he
will get away," said the guide; "hold a little higher
on him this time." As my gun was still resting on
the limb of the juniper, I soon had the crosshairs covering a spot on his white side about two inches below
the top of his wither, and almost simultaneously with
the report of the gun the great deer dropped on both
knees and rolled over, dying before we reached him.
On our way to where he lay we both counted our
steps, and as it was slightly down grade, they would
average fully three feet. The guide counted 296
steps to where he got the first shot, and the writer
had 290; and we both counted twenty-five steps to
where he got his last ball. This was good shooting,

and with the writer would have been an impossibility without the aid of a rest and the telescope sight.

Thus far all was very satisfactory; but when we came to examine the antlers of our stag we were mortified to find the right brow antler broken off, which rendered the specimen useless. We quickly removed his hide and retraced our steps to Grandfather's Lookout, to find the rest of our party gone, we knew not where. But inasmuch as it was not our party we were looking for, we at once brought the glass to focus on the landscape below us, and soon located another herd of caribou. We were sure Kep and the Kid were on the slope somewhere, though farther west of us. They could, as we afterwards learned, see us as well as the deer, and knew from our actions we had also sighted the quarry—in fact, they saw us enter the thick growth of trees which covered the slope for some distance below the highest point. The deer were coming up the slope at an angle and in open ground, in the direction of where Kep and the Kid were lying flat on their bellies, expecting that in case we did not get a chance at the stag, which from all appearances had the finest head of any we had thus far seen or killed, they might stop him as he was coming their way.

The herd was scattered about promiscuously, while

the stag would walk slowly along for twenty-five or thirty yards, then stop for two or three minutes apparently to rest, paying no attention to his surroundings. In the meantime we had succeeded in getting to the edge of the cover just as he stopped on a little hummock, with his great white broadside toward us. I had just time to get the cross lines located by quick work, fearing that he would start again, and thereby induce our friends to shoot in case they were in range. At the report of the gun he twitched, shook his massive head, turned square round to the right, and walked briskly down the hill about two rods, when he stopped, offering a quartering shot, which he got promptly—the second ball entering his right side just back of his right front leg, and lodging just under the skin at the point of the left shoulder, breaking him down. Distance, 150 yards. As soon as he fell the two concealed hunters broke cover and came running at full speed, shouting like Comanches after a successful ambush. After the post mortem the jury agreed without a dissenting voice upon the following verdict :

1st. That the deceased had the largest and finest head they had ever seen.

2d. That he would weigh not less than 600 pounds.

3d. That he had a just right to the title of

and that kings and other potentates were beneath him in all respects, and likely to remain there. Here are his antler measurements :

Length of right beam from hair to tip......42	Inches.
Length of left beam from hair to tip........41½	"
Tip to tip...32¼	"
Spread, centre to centre.......................37¾	"
Circumference of right beam at hair........ 6	"
Circumference of left beam at hair.......... 6½	"
Points on right horn...............32 }........47	"
Points on left horn...............15 }	
Breadth of right palm........................... 7½	"
Breadth of left palm........................... 6½	"
Circumference of entire rack.........11 feet 9	"
Diameter of space occupied by rack..4 "	

Several old Indian and Newfoundland hunters who saw this head were unanimous in the opinion that they had never seen a more perfect or larger one; and the writer is free to say that he believes it is to-day the largest and most perfect woodland caribou head in America, basing his opinion on specimens carefully examined wherever an opportunity was offered, including those at the Columbian Exposition and the Sportsman's Exhibition recently held in Madison Square Garden, New York.

13

LE BUFFE AND THE EMPEROR.

Le Buffe and the writer took careful measurements of the "Emperor," as well as several photographic negatives, when we removed the skin and carried it to the Lookout while the Kid, coached by Kepler, slipped up upon and killed a very fine, unusually white stag which they found feeding in an open or clear patch in a clump of jack-pines, not more than a mile from our temporary camp. This completed his score, and he was well satisfied with his first attempt at large game shooting, as the walls of his residence in Burlington, N. J., will finely illustrate, and where all sportsmen will be heartily welcomed by "The Kid."

Sunday, October 28th. Thermometer 35; high wind from west. Started to complete skinning out the deer, cleaning up the heads and carrying them to the Lookout ready for the carriers, who were expected in the morning. Sighted a herd of deer, coming on the main trail, which passed through the opening where most of our specimens in this section were killed. Le Buffe and the writer succeeded in reaching a scrubby cedar near where the deer crossed the water-way which separated the open slope from the barren hills further west.

THE FEET OF THE EMPEROR.

THE AUTHOR AND HIS PRIZE, THE EMPEROR.

We had just dropped on our knees when the does
and young stags began to file past within thirty yards
of us, and as usual an old stag brought up the rear in
company with a fine antlered doe separating just before they came up—the stag passing to our left about

thirty yards and the doe about the same distance to the right, where most of the herd had just passed. They walked slowly along, stopping every now and then, and as they approached to a point nearly on a line with us we could examine their antlers carefully, Le Buffe examining the stag on the left, while the writer scrutinized the doe on the right. Both had perfect antlers; in short, they were just what we wanted. When this was decided I covered carefully the stag on my left, fired and killed, then swung my gun round to my right and before the doe could recover from her surprise I had made a double and both of the magnificent deer were dead almost at our feet. We broke cover and the rest of the herd galloped off at a rate that would do credit to a broncho under a cowboy.

The balance of the day was spent in getting our trophies in shape for the carriers, who were expected in the morning at an early hour.

Monday, October 29th. Thermometer 30; windy. As the principal actor in a drama is not the best judge of the play, the writer will give way to Mr. Kepler's notes of the day:

"Morning crisp and cold, and made our blood tingle as we broke quarter-inch ice and washed in the little pond just below our temporary camp. While

"biling the kittle" we spied a big stag, and as the
Doctor was entitled to one stag more, he and Le Buffe
went out to the marsh after him. They intercepted
him all right, but as all heads were now measured by
the "Emperor's" he was allowed to pass by. After
finishing breakfast we concluded to pack up and return to our main camp, and make ready to turn our

LEAVING GRANDFATHER'S LOOKOUT.

faces toward salt water. Williams and Sanders had just arrived to help carry out, and after all hands had loaded up with all they thought they could carry, we got under way about 10 A. M., strung out in regular Indian fashion, headed for the Big Marsh—frequently stopping on the way to rest, talk and live over the great sport we had enjoyed in the locality we had just left.

"When about halfway to camp and just as we were rounding a point of one of the many wooded islands in the marsh, Indian Jim, who was in the lead, threw down his pack, dropped to his knees, and sung out, 'Oh! I see deer.' And there in full view, about 300 yards distant, was a herd of about thirty. Some were lying down, others feeding, and a few seemingly on the alert for danger—notably several barren does. Among them were two fine stags, one with a beautiful pair of antlers towering above the rest as they gleamed in the bright sunlight. As there were seven of us in the party we had to be particularly careful not to attract their attention; so we quickly crawled into the edge of a little thicket close by for cover. 'Who wants a stag?' said Le Buffe. 'I do,' said the Doctor; 'you and the Kid take cover to the right, get below them, and I will shoot the best one as they run past us.' 'Follow me close, then,' said Le Buffe, and the two started on a circle, while we all stood within a few feet of each other and enjoyed watching the hunters and game from our concealment. They had good cover most of the way, and fair footing, but in order to get within fair range had to do some close work; but finally they succeeded in worming themselves through the marsh and chaparral to the edge of cover nearest the deer.

"At this juncture we noticed that the big stag suspected something wrong, as he tossed his head in the air and faced the point from which we expected to see smoke followed by a report of the Kid's gun. 'If John shoots at that fellow and misses him, and he comes this way, I will down him sure—see if I don't,' said the Doctor, as he settled himself and fondled his Winchester. A moment later the Kid fired and scored a miss. Instantly the whole herd were in motion and on the alert; but not sure from whence the noise came they appeared uncertain as to what direction to run; but another shot and another miss put them in a full run, and as was supposed right in our direction. 'Now,' said the Doctor, 'I will show him he can't fool with me like he did with the Kid.'

"What a beautiful sight, as they rushed past at full speed about eighty yards distant, in the open marsh.

EXHIBITION STAG.

'Here he comes!' was shouted by all. Bang! went the Doctor's gun, and down went the stag; but up again in an instant and under way with the rest of the herd. Bang! again went the rifle, and down he went promptly as before; but full of game, the noble animal struggled to his feet, but only had time to make a few wicked jumps when the Doctor hit him the third time, the ball passing through his spine. All present agreed that it was the finest exhibition of rifle marksmanship in the field they had ever seen, and congratulations were the order of the day."

We secured the beautiful head of the "Exhibition Stag," and took up our line of march for camp, where we arrived in good shape before night, well satisfied with our trip to Grandfather's Lookout.

Tuesday, October 30th. Thermometer 25; windy. To-day all hands busy skinning out heads and getting them ready for transportation. Sent two carriers out to head of West Pond with heavy loads of heads, antlers and head skins, topped off with such articles of household and kitchen furniture as we could spare. These faithful men left camp with their heavy loads about sunrise, and returned to camp just at dark the same day.

Wednesday, October 31st. Thermometer 32; clear. All busy taking care of our trophies. No hunting done, though quite a number of deer were seen crossing the Big Marsh. This was a charming day.

Thursday, November 1st. Thermometer 32; clear. As the writer was entitled to one more doe, and was desirous of securing a fawn if possible to complete his

KEPLER'S SPECIMENS.

family of reindeer, viz., "The Emperor," cow, "Exhibition Stag," and five-months' old calf—all hands took a walk to the South Hills, where the Kid and Indian Jim had their red-letter day, where the author fortunately killed a fawn which completed his family of specimens as shown on front cover page. We found where a large bear had eaten half of one of the

ARRIVING AT THE FOOT OF WEST POND.

stags killed by the Kid, and had dragged the great deer several feet, showing that he must have been of good size. The conditions were very favorable for a forty-pound trap and about three days' time which without doubt would have furnished some more sport and a fine pelt.

Friday, November 2d. Thermometer 32; clear. Sent the carriers out with three loads. All hands working on skins and heads, getting ready to go out on Sunday. Scattered deer in sight all day. "Deer on the ma'sh" causes no excitement now; three weeks ago things were different. Then every fellow grabbed his gun, got the other fellows' boots or shoes on, and ran with bated breath to the edge of cover.

Sunday, November 4th. Thermometer 35; raining, but cleared off beautifully, and at 9 A. M., after caching the stove and most of our kitchen furniture, we bade adieu to our camp on the Big Marsh and turned our faces toward salt water, arriving at our caché one and a-half miles west of the head of West Pond at 4 P. M., where we camped for the night.

Monday, November 5th. Thermometer 33; windy. Left camp at 8.30 A. M., and soon reached the head of West Pond with whole outfit. Owing to the high wind, the water was so rough that we were detained about two hours, regarding the trip hazardous with

HUGGING THE SOUTH SHORE OF WEST POND.

STUCK ON THE ROCKS AT DEVIL'S ELBOW.

our heavily-laden canoes. Finally made the foot of the pond in safety by hugging the south shore, and after experiencing some difficulty at the "Devil's Elbow," on West Pond Brook between the foot of the pond and the head of Hall's Bay, arriving at our guide's cabin at 3 P. M.

Here we met a disappointment at not receiving letters from home, which confirmed our suspicions as to

MISTAKE NO. 5.

From some correspondence had with a Mr. White, mail agent between Whitbourne and the terminus of the railroad, we were induced to cause our mail to be directd to his care, supposing that there was a mail route from Norris' Arm, via. Pilley's Island, to the Hall's Bay postoffice, and that we would thus receive mail as often as we could send out to the head of the bay. In consequence of this mistake, we had no word from home from the day we sailed until our return. Our folks had telegrams from us, however, from Halifax, St. John's and Pilley's Island on our way north, and on our return to Pilley's Island on our homeward journey.

Sportsmen visiting this country will do well to beware of inducements held out to go via. the railroad from St. John's. If fine sport and large antlers are

desired, "follow your leader and fear no danger."
Take the *Silvia* at New York direct for Pilley's Island. Have your mail matter directed in care of
Richard Le Buffe, to Hall's Bay P. O., Wolf Cove,
Notre Dame Bay, N. F., and Mrs. Brown, the affable
postmistress, and her daughters will as opportunity
offers send them to Mr. Le Buffe's ranch, where they
can be called for by the carriers as they have occasion
to return to the caché at the head of West Pond. Arrangements can also be made with Mr. Herbert, the
gentlemanly postmaster at Pilley's, to send any important telegrams to the camp on the Big Marsh.
The telegraph office for this section is not at Pilley's,
but a few miles further north, at Little Bay Mine,
and ten words cost $1.75 to Philadelphia, Pa., U. S. A.

Tuesday, November 6th. Thermometer 31; threatening. Le Buffe, Indian Jim and the writer left at an
early hour for Wolf Cove, six miles up the bay, in a
small rowboat, to secure a sailing yacht to convey us to
Pilley's Island; while Kep and the Kid unpacked the
head skins, verified the tags or labels on each and arranged them in, over and about Le Buffe's storehouse,
which stood on the edge of the bank fronting the cabin.
In this connection it might be well to state that it is important that every specimen should be carefully
marked and numbered, and for that purpose the wri-

CURING THE HIDES AND HEADS AT LE BUFFE'S STOREHOUSE.

ter was prepared with good strong paper tags with
eyelets, similar to those used by express companies
and general shippers of merchandise. These tags if
plainly marked with a lead pencil, will resist moisture
much better than ink, and no difficulty will be experienced from getting the specimens mixed up. We
returned by 3 P. M., with the yacht, in a storm of
rain and wind; and in consequence of this there was
but little accomplished except securing a means of
transportation up the bay to Pilley's Island.

Wednesday November 7th. Thermometer 32; blowing a terrific gale from the northwest all day. Managed to load some of our plunder; but as the water was so wild that it was with difficulty that we kept the yacht from dragging her anchors, the idea of sailing was abandoned until the storm was abated.

Thursday, November 8th. Thermometer 32; clear and pleasant. As the troubled waters had subsided, we set sail at an early hour and arrived at Pilley's at 12 M., in good shape, where we were welcomed by Mr. Herbert, with whom we engaged quarters until our ship should sail. After settling with our yacht captain and the hands necessary to run the same, we found that the whole bill footed up $30.00—just $20.00 more than it should have cost us, had we done as it is to be hoped others will, viz., engage Capt. Colburn to meet them at the head of Hall's Bay with the *Nipkin* on a certain day, and make it a point to be there ready to embark. This was mistake No. 6.

We at once proceeded to pack our trophies for transportation, and were materially assisted by Mr. Herbert, who furnished three large packing boxes into which we packed our heads, headskins, tent and other large articles which we would not need on the voyage home.

WE WANT TO GO HOME.

The next question to disturb our slumbers was, when would we get a vessel going south? The steamer *Avalon*, a large English vessel (See cut, page 25) known as a tramp belonging to the Red Cross Line, commanded by Capt. E. M. Cox, was loading pyrites for Boston. The steamer *Silvia*, upon which we expected to sail for New York, was looked for daily; but inasmuch as she could not load till the *Avalon* left her dock, we began at once to open negotiations with Capt. Cox to land us in Boston on our home trip, for which point he expected to sail direct not later than Tuesday, the thirteenth, which would get us home at least five days ahead of the *Silvia*.

Friday, November 9th. Thermometer 32; clear and pleasant. This was a lovely day. Spent a very pleasant evening with Capt. Cox at Mr. Herbert's in company with friends of the family, playing Nap and listening to fine music rendered by Mr. Herbert and his estimable wife and daughter. Finished packing our trophies, and received a final answer from Capt. Cox, who agreed to take us; but as he was not allowed to provide accommodations for passengers, he said it would be necessary for us to ship as seamen at one shilling a day, and pay one dollar a day each for our board, with the verbal understanding that we should desert the ship at Boston. Our four days' wait at Pilley's Island were pleasantly spent, and would have been much more enjoyable had it not been for

MISTAKE NO. 7.

We had left our trunks at St. John's which contained our travelling clothes, as well as some presents for the loved ones at home. However, we had prepared a letter of instructions to one of our many new-made friends at St. John's, Mr. J. B. Howson, Esq., to forward our baggage. While in our quandary, on the eleventh the *Silvia* steamed in.

THE SILVIA WAITING IN PILLEY'S ISLAND HARBOR.

On the 12th our cases—one containing five pairs of antlers and five headskins, directed to that master of his profession, Mr. A. H. Wood, taxidermist, of Painted Post, N. Y.; one to J. W. Davis, Burlington, N. J., and the third to the writer at Lancaster, Pa., were stowed away in the hold of the great steel steamer, together with 3,000 tons of pyrites ore; the hatches were clamped down, and on Tuesday morning, just as we were about to hoist anchor, the coast steamer *Virginia Lake* hove in sight, bound for St. John's. Things were beginning to be interesting. It would require three days to load the *Silvia* (perhaps four), and three days for the *Virginia Lake* to reach St. John's. Mr. Kepler, always magnanimous, and full of ways and means as Newfoundland is of caribou, ptarmigan and codfish, said as he stood upon the dock: "Well, boys, though we have made arrangements for having our baggage forwarded to New York, your time at home is more valuable than mine; you have business to look after, I have none; I will go on the *Virginia Lake* to St. John's, and be ready for the *Silvia* when she comes, and we will be sure nothing will happen to our baggage. I will not report for duty on the *Avalon*, then I need not desert at Boston." We exchanged bon-voyage, and both ships sailed out of the harbor at the same time—he going south and we north, through the Straits of Belle Isle, along the shores of Labrador, which were covered with snow, and completely around the west coast of Newfoundland, through the Gulf of St. Law-

COAST OF LABRADOR AS SEEN FROM SHIP IN STRAITS OF BELLE ISLE OPPOSITE AMOUR'S POINT.

rence, past Cape Breton Island, across the Bay of Fundy, and down to Boston, where we arrived at 8 P. M., Monday, November 19th, 1894. The rest of the journey home was, of course, an every-day affair. Mr. Kepler had a pleasant voyage, arriving four days later.

THE CARIBOU AND HIS HABITS.

Though the preceding pages have not been written from the standpoint either of historian or naturalist, it may not be considered amiss to note in detail some of the habits of the noble game which formed the principal subject of the work, and led the author and his friends to visit the distant island.

The North American Caribou, *Rangifer Tarandus*, is the only member of the deer family whose females have horns. This peculiarity has led to the impression with many that *all* doe caribou possess these appendages, which is far from being correct—the fact being that such are the exceptions, not the rule. While we saw during our stay in the White Hills over nine hundred of these noble animals by actual count, we were at one time fearful that all would not get a specimen of the female bearing horns. Like the stags, they shed their horns once a year, though much later in the season. Their antlers are usually quite regular, and about the same size in all specimens. The caribou is powerfully built, with deep broad shoulders, short neck, short clean large-boned legs and broad feet. In the late fall and winter they are almost white, with bluish spots on the sides which give them a dappled gray appearance. The hair is finer, more flexible and less brittle than that of any other member of the deer family, and beneath the hair is a thick mat of fur. Beautiful and serviceable robes are made of the skins.

The woodland caribou are very susceptible to domestication, and make a valuable substitute for dogs in drawing loads over the ice and snow. The writer saw a yearling on board the steamer *Virginia Lake* which had been captured in Red Indian Lake but ten days previous. It was perfectly tame and docile, and took food from the hand without a sign of timidity.

These deer when frightened seldom jump or run, but go off at a lively gallop until they think themselves out of harm's way, when they drop into a fast trot; but soon stop, turn half round, presenting a broadside to the point from which they were frightened, and in a minute or two "about face" and present the other side. If not entirely satisfied as to the cause of their alarm they will often slowly retrace their steps—led usually by a barren doe—and thereby get themselves into trouble.

Where a marsh is of considerable width, through which several trails pass, and the hunter's convenience makes it desirable that the deer take a particular path, all that is necessary is to tie a handkerchief or some similar object to the end of a stick and place it near the junction of the "leads." When the herd comes along, the leader soon discovers the flag and gives the alarm, they all line themselves up, take a good look at the mysterious fluttering object, and take the road which leads to danger.

Their senses of smell and hearing are very acute, but their vision seems defective in distinguishing objects. If a man in a dead-grass colored suit stands perfectly still in the open marsh, they will walk close up to him before (apparently) they are able to distinguish him from a stump or some other object. While they invariably prefer to travel over the open marsh or barrens, when wounded they immediately run for cover; and once within a Newfoundland thicket, the chances are nine in ten they cannot be found.

They are very tenacious of life, and the missile must strike either in or close to the spine or heart, or through both shoulders, as otherwise they are likely to get away. The calf whose head is shown on cover ran three hundred yards after receiving a 40–65 ball through the body just back of the heart.

Here we must leave the caribou to the further acquaintance of those whose fancy leads them in pursuit of the nobler game of our continent. The heads of the principal specimens mentioned in our record

look down upon us from the walls of our home, re-
newing daily the pleasure we found in the pursuit.
Go and do likewise.

THE MICMAC INDIANS.

As reference has been made in the preceding chap-
ters to the Micmacs of Newfoundland, a few words
about them may not be out of place, as they are the
only Indian inhabitants. They belong to the eastern
branch of the Algonquin family, representatives of
which are also found in Nova Scotia, New Brunswick
and Lower Canada. Some thirty families of them
are located around Hall's Bay, and compose about all
on the island. They live in houses like the white men,
speak a little broken English, cultivate small patches
of ground, and eke out a livelihood by fishing and
hunting. They are all Roman Catholics, and in front
of their cemetery on the north shore of Hall's Bay the
cross and a totem-pole stand side by side, and are
guarded with jealous care. Many of these people are
afflicted with tuberculosis of the throat and lungs, from
which cause there are a number of deaths every year.
Notwithstanding his attempts at civilized life, this
member of the aboriginal race is moving towards the
extinction which seems to be the fate of the red man
in every portion of the new world.

CONCLUSION.

And now, about to lay down the pen, as we glance backward by way of farewell to the little book, there crowd upon us pleasant reminiscences of the people among whom we spent those autumn days, so full of pleasure and of incident. We came among them strangers, we left them friends; should we not be tempted back again by the recollection of this visit, at least the friendships formed will not be suffered to lapse, if the islanders reciprocate our feeling toward them, as we have every reason to expect. In this feeling is an element of sympathy which we trust may awaken the same in the heart of the reader. These people of the north have for decades been making a heroic struggle not only against nature's forces, but against the colder and more cruel hand of oppression, moved by soulless greed; and last and worst, against the corruption among themselves induced by the example set them in their treatment by the mother country. But the corruptionists are a small minority; the honest masses will slough them off, and we feel safe in predicting for them a brighter future.

What are the grounds of our belief? First, the seemingly inexhaustible bounty of nature in the waters surrounding them, the undeveloped riches of soil and mine, the elastic spirit shown wherever the smallest opportunity is given for improvement, undaunted by repeated applications of the English "wet blanket," and last and most promising, the almost universal desire for free institutions.

Will the deliverance come in the form of annexation to the great American Republic? Such is their hope, and also that of the writer. He may as well confess here that a confederation of American states from Greenland over to Behring Straits, and southward to Cape Horn, would be none too large for his ideal; but he cannot hope to see that, since the years of Methuselah are no longer vouchsafed to man. But he is not so sure that he may not hold out long enough to hunt the caribou in the American State of Newfoundland.

Whether we shall see it or no, let our last word in taking leave of the reader express once more the hope that instead of a European dependency, the twentieth century may early greet our friends of Newfoundland as in the fullest sense American citizens.

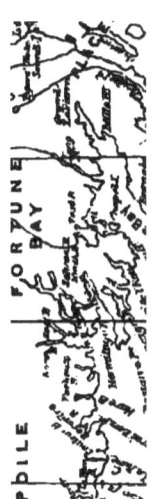

www.ingramcontent.com/pod-product-compliance
Lightning Source LLC
Chambersburg PA
CBHW020606030726
47497CB00007B/2108